The Healthcare Fix

The Healthcare Fix

Universal Insurance for All Americans

Laurence J. Kotlikoff

The MIT Press
Cambridge, Massachusetts
London, England

MIT Press books may be purchased at special quantity discounts for business or sales promotional use. For information, please e-mail special _sales@mitpress.mit.edu or write to Special Sales Department, The MIT Press, 55 Hayward Street, Cambridge, MA 02142.

This book was set in Stone Sans and Stone Serif by The MIT Press. Printed and bound in the United States of America.

Library of Congress Cataloging-in-Publication Data

Kotlikoff, Laurence J.
The healthcare fix : universal insurance for all Americans / Laurence J. Kotlikoff.
    p. ; cm.
Includes bibliographical references and index.
ISBN 978-0-262-11314-4 (hardcover : alk. paper)
1. National health insurance—United States.   2. Insurance, Health—Government policy—United States.   3. Medically uninsured persons—United States.   4. Health services accessibility—United States.
5. Medical care, Cost of—United States.   6. Health care Reform—United States.   7. Medicare.   8. Medicaid.   I. Title.
[DNLM: 1. Insurance, Health—United States.   2. Health Care Reform—United States.   3. Medically Uninsured—United States.   4. Universal Coverage—United States. W 275 AA1 K797h 2007]

RA412.2.K68   2007
368.4'200973—dc22   2007028956

10   9   8   7   6   5   4   3   2   1

For my wonderful family and our nation's marvelous healthcare practitioners

Contents

The Healthcare Fix

1 | Driving off a Cliff

The status quo, we're conditioned to believe, is the safe bet, the conservative option, the riskless alternative. But when the status quo involves driving off a cliff, maintaining course is the risky, radical, indeed suicidal choice. The United States is now engaged in precisely this behavior: perpetuating a suicidal status quo. Its policies, primarily those connected with Medicare, Medicaid, and the rest of the healthcare system, are driving the country to fiscal, financial, and economic ruin. The only question is when the crash will occur and who will be in the passenger seats.

Financial markets appear to have no inkling of what's coming. But these markets often need a two-by-four across the forehead to come to their senses. This is one of those times. Long-term U.S. Treasury yields are remarkably low when, in fact, the United States is facing bankruptcy and will surely end up printing vast quantities of money to meet its bills. This prospect should be driving interest rates through the roof. *Bankruptcy* is a strong word and not to be used lightly. It's particularly hard to justify when the economy is growing well, the deficit is shrinking as a share of national income, and the stock market is rising. But economic growth and rising stock markets don't preclude economic collapse. Recall that the Great Depression followed the Roaring Twenties. And consider Argentina's decade of outstanding growth and stock market appreciation prior to its economy going belly-up in 2002 thanks to a financial crisis precipitated by a fiscal crisis. As with physical health, when it comes to economic health, what you don't see can hurt you, even kill you. What the politicians and public don't see, or don't want to see, are the enormous future fiscal obligations facing the U.S. government. These obligations are gargantuan for two reasons. First, we have 77 million baby boomers heading inexorably into retirement and relatively few workers coming up behind them. When the last of them retires, in roughly twenty-five years, we'll have twice the number of retirees we have today, but only 18 percent more workers to help support them. Second, in twenty-five years, the combined benefit payment to retired baby boomers through the Medicare, Medicaid (state as well as federal) and Social Security programs, which I denote the MMS benefit, will average well over $30,000 measured in today's dollars.[1] Thirty thousand dollars is incredibly high. It's more than three-quarters of current per capita income, the standard measure of our nation's living standard![2]

Could a time come when Uncle Sam provides the elderly, on average, benefits that exceed three-quarters of per capita income? Yes. In fact, Uncle Sam is already doing just that. Today's MMS payment per elderly is $30,304, which is 79 percent of the current $38,367 level of per capita income.[3]

Uncle Sam wasn't always this generous. In 1965 the MMS payment to the elderly averaged only 28 percent of per capita income. But over time Uncle Sam has opened his wallet. In 1980 he handed the elderly average MMS benefits equal to 63 percent of per capita income. By 1995 his generosity had reached 76 percent. And today it's 79 percent.

The Giver Who Keeps On Giving

Clearly Uncle Sam is on a roll, and there's every reason to expect his largess to continue. Indeed, in adding prescription drug coverage (Part D) to Medicare, Uncle Sam helped ensure that MMS benefits at the end of this decade will equal 83 percent of Americans' standard of living. And based on the intermediate projections of the Congressional Budget Office (CBO), the MMS payment will grow to 88 percent of per capita income by 2020, 91 percent by 2030, 98 percent by 2040, and 106 percent by 2050.

Today's fifty-year-olds were born in 1957, smack dab in the middle of the baby boom. In 2035, they'll be smack dab in the middle of their retirements. Their MMS benefit in that year, measured in today's dollars, will average $50,540, two-thirds higher than today's average.

Multiply 77 million baby boomers by $50,540, and you arrive at an annual aggregate MMS payment in 2035 of $3.9 trillion. That's one colossal amount. To put it in perspective, it's 30 percent of our current $13.3 trillion gross domestic product (GDP).

Of course, twenty-five years from now is a long time, and our economy will be much larger than it is today. But it won't take twenty-five years for the total MMS costs to become exceptionally large compared to GDP; indeed, they're already very large.

Back in 1965 MMS costs represented 2.5 percent of GDP. Today they represent 9.4 percent. In a decade, they'll constitute 11.9 percent. By 2020 they'll be 13.6 percent. In 2035 they'll represent 18.4 percent. In 2050, they'll total 21.8 percent.

These programs aren't free. They are paid for with payroll and income taxes. Hence, scaling up MMS spending relative to the size of the economy by a factor of 2.3 (21.8 divided by 9.4) between now and midcentury means scaling up the tax rates needed to pay for these programs by a huge factor as well.

The main cost culprits are Medicare and Medicaid. The reason is simple: their benefits levels have risen and are expected to continue to rise much more rapidly than social security's. Today Medicare plus Medicaid expenditures represent just over half of total MMS spending. But by 2035, the Medicare plus Medicaid share of MMS spending will reach two-thirds. By 2050 it will reach 70 percent.

If moving from spending 9.4 percent of our nation's output on the elderly to spending 21.8 percent sounds problematic, it is. But given the way Medicare and Medicaid are structured, we'll be incredibly lucky to get away with this size increase. The CBO's intermediate projection, which entails the rise in the MMS-GDP spending share to 21.8 percent by midcentury, assumes that Medicare and Medicaid benefits per beneficiary grow in the future at a rate that is only 1.0 percentage point higher than the growth rate of per capita GDP. That's a truly heroic assumption given that over the past three-plus decades, the differential has been not 1.0 percentage point but 2.6 percentage points.[4]

When the CBO assumes higher spending on Medicare and Medicaid (a 2.5 percentage point rather than a 1.0 percentage point differential), the MMS benefit level rises from its current 79 percent share of per capita income to 90 percent in 2015, 96 percent in 2020, 107 percent in 2030, 129 percent in 2040, and *159* percent in 2050. Total MMS spending rises from 9.4 percent of GDP today, to 20.5 in 2035, to 28.5 percent in 2050.

Paying the Piper

Can our country afford to allocate an ever increasing share of its output to the care and sustenance of the elderly? Clearly no. The cost of paying for this largess, given everything else the country has on its plate, far exceeds the capacity or willingness of current and future taxpayers to pay.

The elderly are surely highly valued. Indeed, they are in many ways revered members of our society. But they are not the majority of the population and never will be, notwithstanding the significant aging of our country. Indeed, according to current projections, the elderly will never constitute more than one-quarter of the population. The rest of the population—the children, teenagers, young adults, and the middle-aged—have their own economic and healthcare needs. And these needs have become more pronounced with the rise in healthcare costs, the ongoing decline in health insurance coverage, and the relative and, in many cases, absolute declines in the real incomes of the poor and the middle class.

Since 1970 the elderly have received, on average, real (measured in today's dollars) Medicare and Medicaid benefit hikes of 4.6 percent per year.[5] At the same time, the workers paying for these benefits have experienced real increases in total compensation per hour of only 1.7 percent per year.[6] In the past fifteen years, the MMS benefit has risen in real terms by almost 52 percent, whereas median household income has risen by less than 12 percent.

Moreover, much of the increase in total compensation per hour has taken the form of higher employer payments for health insurance, which hardly feels like getting a raise. Leaving out employer-paid health insurance premium payments and other fringe benefits reveals something truly striking: workers have seen their real wages decline over time at the same time the elderly have been enjoying benefit increases. Average real hourly wages are now actually 3.4 percent lower than they were in 1970. In comparison, the real MMS benefit is 200 percent larger today than it was in 1970.[7]

As the elderly have sat back and enjoyed ever greater health-care benefits—extra benefits that will have to be paid for by today's and tomorrow's workers—working families have experienced more and more difficulty protecting themselves financially from adverse health events. Today 47 million Americans, almost all of working age or younger, have no health insurance. In 1987 the number of uninsured was 32 million. Thus, in two decades we've seen almost a 40 percent rise in the number of uninsured.[8]

Think about 47,000,000. It's an enormous number on its own terms, but also relative to the number of young and middle-aged Americans. Since there are 267 million Americans under age sixty-five, we're talking about almost one in five working-age and younger Americans having no health insurance. Lots of our uninsured compatriots are very young; they are children.

Indeed, more than 8 million of America's uninsured are below age nineteen.[9]

What happens when uninsured folks show up at the emergency room with no medical insurance? It used to be they'd be seen and sent the bill later. That's no longer the case. Today many hospitals require that the uninsured charge their treatment. This explains why one in five low- and middle-income households now report charging major medical expenses on their credit cards.[10] When these households fail to pay their hospital bills, it's not the hospital they stick with the bills. It's the credit card companies. And the credit card companies aren't in the habit of getting stuck. They have no compulsion against charging fantastically high interest rates on outstanding balances and forcing delinquents into bankruptcy.

What a marvelous country we live in. All of a sudden your gallbladder goes south, you are in terrible pain, you barely make it to the hospital, you have surgery, and after the anesthesia wears off, you're presented with a staggering bill that puts you into bankruptcy and hands over your house to the credit card company.

Why Remain Uninsured?

Why, you might ask (if you aren't currently paying for your own health insurance), would anyone remain uninsured if that choice entails so much financial risk? The answer is that buying health insurance on one's own (outside of an employer's plan) is astronomically expensive. Today Blue Cross Blue Shield is charging a family of four living in Boston $19,757 to buy a plan with full coverage. United Health is charging $45,166, an amount larger than U.S. per capita income.[11]

The average premium costs to employers of insuring the health expenses of their employees and their families is lower but still incredibly high: over $12,000 per worker for large firms with 200 plus employees. Small businesses with fewer than 200 employees aren't so lucky: they pay 80 to 90 percent of the price charged to individual purchasers of health insurance.[12] If all this weren't bad enough, rising healthcare costs are driving American companies broke. Collectively, our nation's firms are now paying some $500 billion annually in employee and retiree health insurance premiums and health expenditure claims (in the case of companies that self-insure).[13] It's no coincidence that Ford Motor Company is spending over $3 billion per year for healthcare for its retirees and current workers, that these costs are rising annually in real terms at roughly 6 percent, and that it is in the process of laying off 40 percent of its workforce.[14] Nor is it a coincidence that General Motors is sitting on a $15 billion healthcare liability.[15]

Most economists would counter that in providing health insurance to its employees, GM, Ford, and other companies are simply paying their workers in a different form, so that rising healthcare expenditures are really coming out of workers' pockets in the form of lower regular wages than would otherwise be the case. There is, surely, much truth to this observation. But what it overlooks is that American companies are engaged in either explicit or implicit long-term contracts with their workers under which they've agreed to bear certain risks, including the risks of paying for rising health insurance premiums (or rising healthcare costs, if they are paying for healthcare directly). Indeed, there are millions of retired autoworkers who are receiving healthcare based on past promises by their firms. Few of the firms paying these healthcare benefits anticipated the type of healthcare inflation we've seen in recent years. They can't lower their retirees' wages because they are already as low as they can get, namely zero. None of these firms have any recourse other than paying for these benefits or reneging on their obligations by either refusing to pay (a perfectly legal option for most companies) or going out of business.

Many employers are starting to wise up and get out of the highly risky business of providing health insurance coverage for their workers. In 2000, 66 percent of nonelderly Americans were covered by employer-based health insurance. Today's figure is 59 percent.[16] Employers that continue to offer health insurance are beginning to renege on their implicit contracts by asking their employees to pay for ever larger shares of the premiums. As a consequence, millions of U.S. workers are declining coverage in their employers' plans.[17] So yes, much of what has the appearance of higher employer costs is starting to come out of the hides of employees. But during this transition period, much is also coming out of the hides of firms that are fulfilling their part of explicit or implicit contractual relationships, leaving them with fewer resources to invest in their operations.

What Can't Go On Can Stop Too Late

Herb Stein, the distinguished economist, used to say, "What can't go on will stop." That's absolutely true. But when it comes to growth in public and private healthcare costs and the effects of this on individual welfare, employers' bottom lines, and our nation's overall finances, what can't go on will stop too late.

Take the MMS benefit. The level of this benefit is already so high that were it simply to remain steady over time at 79 percent of per capita income, the aging of our population would, by midcentury, raise the share of GDP spent on MMS from 9.3 percent to 14.7 percent. That's 5.4 more percentage points of GDP. To put this figure in perspective, total FICA tax revenues (total receipts from employer plus employee Social Security Old Age Insurance Disability and Health Insurance contributions) currently amount to only 6.4 percent of GDP. So just the aging of our population will eventually require close to a doubling of our current 15.3 percent combined employee-employer payroll tax unless we make provision in advance.

The Overall Fiscal Gap

Given a projection of future MMS spending as well as all other government expenditures, how does one tally up total future spending and compare the size of this fiscal bill with all the tax and other receipts the government can expect to collect in the short, medium, and long runs? The answer is called the *fiscal gap*, which equals the value in the present (the *present value*) of all the government's projected future expenditures, including servicing the national debt, minus the present value of all the government's future taxes.[18]

The U.S. fiscal gap, now close to $70,000,000,000,000, corresponds to roughly $230,000 per American man, woman, and child. Eliminating this fiscal gap will require radical changes in our nation's fiscal policy, starting with sea changes in the way the government provides healthcare to Medicare and Medicaid participants. But reforming Medicare and Medicaid (which is absolutely critical) will do nothing to deal with our two other healthcare crises: the fact that 47 million Americans are uninsured and that exploding health insurance costs are driving companies out of business.

What's needed and what this book offers is a universal healthcare plan that provides a single fix—*the* healthcare fix—for each of these interrelated problems. I call the solution the *Medical Security System (MSS)*. It's simple to state and easy to understand.

• MSS provides every American with an annual voucher to buy a basic healthcare plan/insurance policy for the year.
• Those with preexisting health conditions receive larger vouchers.
• The government sets the overall voucher budget in line with what's affordable.

Designing this fix to our healthcare problems is simple. What's hard is getting politicians to face up to the fiscal realities. As I write this book, the major presidential candidates are advocating policies that address only one of our three healthcare problems: the 47 million Americans with no health insurance. Their "solutions" for the uninsured entail sticking them in what can only be described as a loser's insurance pool in which participants receive third-rate insurance coverage that entails significant copayments, high deductibles, exclusions, and ceilings on coverage. Since this population includes a disproportionate number of poor people, and since the poor, as a rule, are in worse health than the rich, the loser's pool has higher-than-average expected healthcare costs. Hence, the insurance companies will provide coverage only if they are compensated at a higher price than they would charge the general population.

To finance this higher price, the candidates propose direct government subsidization as well as forcing all employers that don't provide health insurance coverage to pay a special fee per worker. The uninsured who don't work, including many very poor people, will be required to buy a health insurance policy. Finally, to limit the size of the loser pool and the costs of the per-loser premium, the candidates propose substantially expanding Medicaid coverage. As for Medicare, they propose no changes.

But worsening Medicaid's finances and letting Medicare's continue to hemorrhage will leave no money for anything else, let alone massive government subsidies for losers' insurance. And rather than help employers exit the health insurance business, these schemes permanently trap all employers in it. Forcing the uninsured poor to pay for their own coverage is not a solution. There is no way to force someone who is poor to buy health insurance, meaning we'll still end up with an army of uninsured when all is said and done.

The Game Plan

Before presenting the Medical Security System, my solution to the healthcare crisis, I need to lay some groundwork. A key task, taken up at the end of this chapter and chapter 2, is to show that the current Medicare and Medicaid systems are driving the nation to the poorhouse. I do so by documenting the incredibly high historical benefit growth rate in these programs and by pointing out that this growth is excessive both on its own terms and by international standards. I also show the extent to which excessive growth in Medicare and Medicaid benefit levels is increasing the fiscal gap and how much taxes will have to be raised or spending on other programs cut to accommodate this growth. Be forewarned: this analysis may scare the daylights out of you. If so, that's good. We all need to understand the extent of this dilemma if we are going to make the tough decisions needed to change direction.

To be sure, my goal is not to write an economics horror novel. It's to lay out the facts and let readers draw their own conclusion. The facts, in the case of the fiscal gap, are not even of my own assembly. Instead they come by way of a very credible source: the U.S. Treasury, whose economists first measured the fiscal gap in 2002. These same economists—Jagadeesh Gokhale (now at the Cato Institute) and Kent Smetters (now at the University of Pennsylvania)—have updated their analysis over time. In discussing the current fiscal gap, I'll be simply reporting their latest findings.[19]

The initial 2002 Treasury study was commissioned by Treasury Secretary Paul O'Neill in consultation with Federal Reserve chairman Alan Greenspan.[20] The study, which showed a $45 trillion gap, was due to be included in the president's 2003 budget. In what was no coincidence, the study was censored by the White House two days after O'Neill was fired by the president. To their lasting credit and the nation's great benefit, Gokhale and Smetters quickly left Treasury and published the study.[21]

Two tax cuts, huge expansions of Medicare and Medicaid, major military and other discretionary spending hikes, and the accrual of three years of interest later, the fiscal gap stands at the aforementioned $70 trillion. That's right: the true measure of our fiscal shortfall rose by 56 percent in just five years. This is an amazing record of fiscal profligacy.

Once one comprehends the magnitude of the U.S. fiscal gap and sees how much Medicare and Medicaid benefit growth contributes to its size, there's only one conclusion to draw: we must stop excessive benefit growth dead in its tracks. The question is how.

Chapter 3 points out that it's essentially impossible to limit growth in Medicare spending and, to a lesser extent, Medicaid spending given the way these programs are structured. This structure has left and will continue to leave the government (state as well as federal) on the hook to pay for the medical care that its Medicare and, to a lesser extent, Medicaid participants wanted and will want rather than for the medical care the government could and can afford.

If we need to scrap our current healthcare system and replace it with something that works for everyone and is affordable, what principles should it satisfy? Chapter 4 answers this question, pointing out that there is a great deal of consensus in the country concerning how each of us should be treated in society. I dub these norms *Principles of American Paternalism* and argue that one can discern these principles by simply looking at policy—how we actually treat people, including people who get sick and can't afford to pay for healthcare. The fact of the matter is we take care of them: we already provide universal healthcare; we just don't call it that.

Chapter 5 examines current and past healthcare reform proposals advanced by the president, other politicians, and state governments to satisfy these principles, but it argues that none gets us to first base in terms of a system that is affordable; they ignore entirely Medicare and seek to expand Medicaid, when both programs are bleeding our nation's finances dry. Chapter 6 provides my simple but radical solution to our three-part healthcare crisis: the Medical Security System. This proposal would scrap Medicare and Medicaid and set up a single health insurance system for everyone in the country. It would eliminate employer-based healthcare insurance and thereby relieve the nation's firms of a liability they can't handle. At first glance, the Medical Security System may seem more expensive than the current system. But the final section of chapter 6 argues that federal and state government is spending so much money on healthcare in so many different ways that simply redirecting all this spending to support the Medical Security System can likely permit us to implement the new system without raising taxes. Chapter 7, the conclusion, recaps the book's central message: we need to come up with a radically new healthcare system that works rather than perpetuate the old one that doesn't. In so doing, we can kill three birds with one stone. First, we can eliminate runaway spending on Medicare and Medicaid by incorporating all their participants and all other Americans in the new Medical Security System, which will operate under a planned and affordable budget.[22] Second, we can provide explicit, rather than implicit, insurance coverage to the 47 million Americans now uninsured. Third, we can get the 800-pound health-insurance-cost gorilla off the backs of America's businesses by providing all Americans, including all American workers, with a new public-private healthcare insurance system.

2 Who's Watching the Shop?

The history of federal spending on Medicare and Medicaid spending on the elderly can best be described as reckless child endangerment. For over four decades, one administration after another has permitted these programs to grow much more rapidly than the economy, while financing this growth on a pay-and-receive basis—with the young paying and the old receiving. And when each cohort of young reaches old age, it's payback time—time to extract as much as possible from contemporaneous young workers.

Hyperbole? Unfortunately not, as this chapter documents. Relative to healthcare growth in other countries and relative to income growth in our country, growth in Medicare and Medicaid spending has been off the chart. And, as I'll discuss at the end of the chapter, the stakes involved in letting this process continue are enormous.

The fee-for-service payment system is the primary contributing factor to the excessive Medicare and Medicaid growth. It has put spending on these programs largely on autopilot. More precisely, the government has positioned itself to be responsible for paying whatever the healthcare delivery system and the Medicare and Medicaid participants using the system collectively decide they want to provide and receive in terms of healthcare services.

Let me explain. The vast majority of Medicare participants and two-fifths of Medicaid participants are receiving healthcare under fee-for-service. Under this system, participants receive the services they want or can cajole out of providers and the government gets to pay the bill, that is, the fee. For example, if you are seventy-three years old and see a rheumatologist for an aching joint, the rheumatologist will bill Medicare, which will cover 80 percent of the fee. The remaining 20 percent is your responsibility or that of your supplemental (major medical) insurer. If you aren't happy with this rheumatologist, you can go see another, and another after that if you want. Why not? Uncle Sam will continue to foot 80 percent of all the bills.

Understanding the fee-for-service system and the failed history of trying to work with it to contain cost is critical for realizing that only radical change in Medicare and Medicaid—indeed, replacing them with something foolproof when it comes to expenditures—will keep these programs from bankrupting the country.

Government Healthcare Spending at Home and Abroad: Who's Going Broke?

Table 2.1 shows two sets of average annual real growth rates for ten member countries of the Organization for Economic Cooperation and Development (OECD) between 1970 and 2002.[1] The second column records growth rates in benefit levels, by which I mean the real levels of government healthcare spending per person at a given age. The third column shows growth rates in real levels of per capita output. The fourth column provides the ratio of the entries in column 2 to those in column 3; that is, it shows how many times higher benefit growth has been compared to per capita output growth.

The age-specific benefit level, as defined here, can rise for two reasons. First, the government can increase the medical goods and services provided to those of a given age group who are enrolled in its healthcare programs. Second, the government can enroll in its programs a larger share of the population at that age.

As table 2.1 shows, real (inflation-adjusted) annual benefit-level growth rates are very high in all ten of the OECD countries considered. They are particularly high in the case of the United States, Spain, and Norway. Norway's 5.04 percent rate is the highest, Spain's 4.63 percent rate is second highest, and the United States's 4.61 percent rate is third highest. Canada recorded the lowest growth rate in benefit levels, namely 2.32 percent. Canada and Sweden are the only countries among the ten with a benefit growth rate below 3.00 percent.

The U.S. 4.61 percent annual real benefit growth rate is 2.29 times higher than the growth rate in its living standard, measured by per capita GDP. The absolute difference between the U.S. benefit and per capita GDP growth rates is 2.60 percentage points. This is huge and far greater than the 1.00 percentage points assumed by the Congressional Budget Office in projecting future Medicare and Medicaid benefit growth.

Table 2.1
Average annual real growth rates in healthcare benefits and per capita GDP, 1970 to 2002

Country	Benefit level	Per capita GDP	Ratio
United States	4.61%	2.01%	2.29
Germany	3.30%	1.54%	2.14
Australia	3.66%	1.76%	2.08
Spain	4.63%	2.34%	1.98
Norway	5.04%	3.06%	1.65
United Kingdom	3.46%	2.11%	1.64
Austria	3.72%	2.44%	1.52
Japan	3.57%	2.44%	1.46
Sweden	2.35%	1.68%	1.40
Canada	2.32%	2.04%	1.14

Source: Christian Hagist and Laurence J. Kotlikoff, "Who's Going Broke? Comparing Healthcare Costs in Ten OECD Countries" (National Bureau of Economic Research, working paper 11833, December 2005).
Note: The growth rates are geometric averages.

Benefit levels have grown faster than living standards in all ten countries, but the United States is at the top (or bottom, depending on your perspective) of the class when it comes to the size of the differential. This has important implications for assessing the relative fiscal health of the United States.

Compare, for example, the United States and Japan. As indicated in table 2.2, both countries are aging, but Japan is aging much more rapidly and extensively. Indeed, thanks to its incredibly low fertility rate of roughly 1.2, Japan's population is already shrinking. By midcentury 37 percent of Japan's population will be age sixty-five or older. In comparison, the U.S. elderly population share will equal only 21 percent. The ratio of 37 to 21 is

Table 2.2
Share of the population age 65 and over

Country	2002	2030	2050	2070
Australia	12.2	20.4	24.0	25.2
Austria	15.5	24.4	29.1	31.1
Canada	13.0	23.6	26.7	27.1
Germany	17.1	26.3	30.6	31.3
Japan	18.0	29.9	36.8	37.7
Norway	15.1	21.0	23.6	24.5
Spain	16.2	24.2	34.0	30.0
Sweden	17.2	25.5	28.5	29.3
United Kingdom	15.9	22.9	26.1	27.3
United States	12.4	19.1	21.3	21.6
Average	14.8	22.6	25.9	25.6

Source: United Nations (2005), *World Population Prospects: The 2002 Revision and World Urbanization Prospects: The 2001 Revision*, Population Division of the Department of Economic and Social Affairs of the United Nations Secretariat, http://esa.un.org/unpp, 20 March 2005; 8:50:27 PM.

1.76, which means Japan's population will be much older than that of the United States and should, other things being equal, face a much bigger long-term fiscal burden for their care.

But other things aren't equal. The other key factor in determining overall healthcare costs is the growth in benefit levels. If the United States and Japan experience for the next forty-four years the same average annual growth rates that they clocked between 1970 and 2002, benefit levels in the United States in 2050 will be 7.26 times higher than they are today. In Japan they'll be only 4.68 times higher. The ratio of 7.26 to 4.68 is 1.55, which is also quite sizable.

Of course, the differential in benefit growth rates could continue beyond 2050. It could also widen over the short and medium term. In fact, there is good reason to expect such a widening. The Japanese government, like all other OECD governments apart from the United States, has direct control over its healthcare expenditures; that is, the government directly funds the hospitals, hires the doctors and nurses, buys the medicines, determines who gets what operations, and so forth. If the Japanese government so desires, it can directly limit spending on healthcare from one day to the next. In the U.S. case, there is no such direct control. To reiterate, Medicare and, to a lesser degree, Medicaid participants effectively decide how much healthcare services they'd like and send most of the bills for these services to Washington. Uncle Sam has no surefire way to turn off the faucet.

The Japanese are now facing intense budgetary pressures. Almost one-fifth of their population is already sixty-five or older, and by midcentury the share will be close to 40 percent. The Japanese government has begun to exercise its direct control over healthcare expenditures and appears serious about bringing an expedient end to benefit growth in excess of growth in per capita GDP.[2] This, no doubt, will entail hiring fewer doctors and nurses, limiting the growth in the pay of healthcare professionals, sanctioning fewer and less expensive new healthcare procedures, liming the purchase and dispensation of new pharmaceuticals, and more. What's true of Japan is also true of other OECD countries. The governments in those countries are all likely to be much more effective over the short and medium terms in limiting their spending on healthcare than the United States.

So what? What's the import of U.S. benefit growth rates out-
stripping most other OECD countries in the future by an even
greater margin? The import is that this factor can readily leave
the United States in the worst long-term fiscal position, as measured by its fiscal gap, of the developed countries. Yes, aging mat-
ters. And yes, compared with other OECD countries, the United
States has a relatively young population and will continue to
over time. But the power of compound growth is staggering and
potentially a much more significant factor than demographics
in determining the relative sizes of countries' fiscal gaps.

Table 2.3 confirms this point. It shows the present value of
government healthcare projections as a share of the present
value of GDP for the ten OECD countries. This analysis fully
incorporates projected demographic changes in each country
and assumes that the historic (1970–2002) benefit growth rates
will prevail for the next four decades; after that, benefit growth
will fall in line with growth in per capita GDP. The calculations
use a 3 percent real discount rate, which seems reasonable given
recent real returns on U.S. inflation-indexed bonds.

Once again we see the United States in a "leadership" position. Its present value government healthcare costs equal 18.8
percent of the present value of each dollar of the nation's projected future output. The size of this figure is astounding in its
own right. In lay terms, it means that the United States is, under
the stated assumptions, on a course to spend close to one-fifth
of all future output (measured in the present) on two healthcare
programs that cover only a minority of the population.

Equally astounding is the top ranking of the United States with
respect to long-term health costs measured as a share of its long-

Table 2.3
Present value of government healthcare expenditures as a percentage of
the present value of GDP

Country	Percent
United States	18.8
Germany	15.0
Australia	13.7
Spain	11.9
Norway	17.2
United Kingdom	11.4
Austria	9.5
Japan	12.9
Sweden	10.6
Canada	11.7

Source: Hagist and Kotlikoff, "Who's Going Broke?"

term output. This is true despite the fact that the United States
has the youngest population among the ten countries over the
long term. Japan, which is the oldest of the ten countries and
will remain so throughout the century, has present value healthcare costs totaling only 12.9 percent of its future output—almost
one-third less than the U.S. figure.

What's the upshot of this international comparison? First,
benefit growth can be more important than demographics in
determining how much Uncle Sam will spend in the future on
healthcare. Second, the United States may be in the worst long-
run fiscal shape (as measured by the ratio of its fiscal gap to GDP)
among the OECD countries because it has had, and may well
continue to have, explosive benefit growth that either outstrips
or far outstrips benefit growth in other developed countries.

Who's to Blame?

The 4.61 percent U.S. annual Medicare and Medicaid benefit growth rate recorded (table 2.1) between 1970 and 2002 is the achievement of five Republican presidents—Nixon, Ford, Reagan, Bush I, and Bush II—and two Democratic presidents—Carter and Clinton—all of whom were nominally watching the shop as money flew out its windows to fund ever higher levels of benefits.

Of course, each year that benefits rose, on average, by 4.61 percent, the benefit increase represented not just a bonus for Medicare and Medicaid participants in that year but in future years as well. The reason is that in this country, benefit increases have never been reversed and likely never will.

Thus, when President Clinton permitted real Medicare benefit levels to rise by 25 percent in his first term in office, he was effectively increasing not just immediate Medicare spending by one-quarter, but the present value of all future expenditures as well. That increase in future obligations was not reported in the president's budget for a good reason. The Clinton administration did just what the Bush II administration had in 2002: it suppressed a long-term fiscal analysis a few weeks before it was to be published in the president's budget.[3] The motivation for the censorship was the same in both cases. First, make sure no one focuses on the true increase in the nation's indebtedness. Second, maintain public focus on the official deficit even though official debt represents less than 10 percent of the overall fiscal shortfall that we adult Americans apparently expect to bequeath to our children.

Bush II is certainly doing nothing to limit growth in health-care spending. Indeed, according to the Government Account-ability Office, the new Medicare Part D prescription drug benefit has a present value cost in excess of $8 trillion. Its introduction is one reason that annual growth in Medicare benefit levels is projected to average 5.52 percent per year over the course of George Walker Bush's eight years of "leadership."

Understanding Growth in Benefit Levels

Clearly the introduction of new types of healthcare coverage, like prescription drug coverage, can play a major role in explain-ing growth in healthcare benefit levels. But there are two other critically important factors. One is a rise in the use of the health-care system and the services it provides. The other is the intro-duction of new services, which are often more advanced and in many cases more costly than their predecessors.[4]

The acquisition of CT scanners in Spain illustrates the role of these other two factors. In 1984 Spain had only 1.6 CT scanners per 1 million inhabitants compared with 11 per million in the United States.[5] By 2001 Spain had 12.3 CT scanners per 1 million inhabitants versus 12.8 in the United States.[6] Having so many more CT scanners meant being able to serve a lot more people. Consequently, there was a huge expansion in CT use in Spain. Japan also expanded its availability and use of medical technol-ogy between 1970 and 2002. In fact, Japan now appears to have the largest number of CTs among the developed countries.[7]

Sometimes new technologies can provide a cheaper solution to an existing medical problem yet still end up costing more money by inducing much greater demand, especially when the government is paying for their use. Health economists David Cutler and Mark McClellan provide a good example of this in their study of angioplasty.[8] They point out that prior to the introduction of angioplasty (roto-rootering one's arteries), heart patients who wanted to have their pipes cleaned (actually replaced) had to undergo painful and risky coronary bypass surgery. Given the pain and risk of the procedure, bypass surgery was used only for those in critical need. But with the advent of angioplasty, which involves much less invasive surgery, the demand for pipe-cleaning shot way up. And so did the collective pipe-cleaning expenditure, much of which, of course, is being paid by Uncle Sam or, should I say, our kids.

Consumer Sovereignty or Fiscal Child Abuse?

As our country has grown richer, we've spent an ever larger share of our output on healthcare services and products. In 1960 the share was just 5 percent; today it's 17 percent.[9] The association of higher incomes with disproportionately higher healthcare spending is evident in table 2.1 as well. The ratios of the ten OECD countries' benefit growth rates to their per capita GDP growth rates range from 1.14 (Canada) to 2.29 (the United States). The average value of this ratio equals 1.73, meaning that for each 10 percent increase in per capita income, there is a 17.3 percent increase in government spending on healthcare.[10]

Many economists view the income-healthcare spending relationship as evidence that healthcare is a "superior good,"[11] that is, a good or service that garners a larger share of expenditures as income rises. The fact that there are superior goods as well as inferior goods, like canned meat, to which nations allocate a smaller fraction of their incomes as their incomes rise, is reflective, to these economists, of consumer preferences and viewed as a legitimate exercise of consumer sovereignty. But what's going on with respect to government healthcare spending cannot simply be viewed as the government acting as the faithful servant of today's households, applying their preferences and exercising their consumer sovereignty. The reason is that current governments are not necessarily spending the incomes of current households. Indeed, given the pay-and-receive manner in which the United States and many other OEDC countries have been financing healthcare spending, one might best characterize what's going on as today's households deciding how to spend on themselves the incomes of tomorrow's households and using governments to implement these decisions.

Stated differently, given the way the United States and other governments do their bookkeeping and discuss their policies, it's hard to know how the cost of paying for a given year's rise in government healthcare spending and, indeed, any other type of government spending will be allocated across generations. Consequently we can't simply view growth in the ratio of government healthcare spending to GDP as a benign process in which today's households decide to allocate a larger share of their higher incomes on existing and improved medical goods and services. Instead we might best consider this process as a manifestation of intergenerational expropriation (the old taking resources from the young) whose full extent is unclear.

Expenditure Growth through Enrollment

Much of the recent growth in total Medicaid spending has arisen owing to growth in enrollment. The government, noticing an ever larger fraction of the population without insurance coverage, has stepped in to provide direct coverage, particularly to households that are not far above the poverty line.[12] Medicare spending growth has also been fueled by enrollment growth, in this case by the inclusion of the disabled and the growth in their numbers. Today there are more than 42 million Medicare enrollees—roughly one-quarter more than in 1990. Our nation now has over 300 million people. Medicare and Medicaid together cover 100 million. This leaves another 200 million Americans who can be added to the rolls by politicians seeking reelection. This potential for expanding enrollment in conjunction with explosive growth in benefits per enrollee, which, as indicated, has been the historic norm, has the potential to expand our nation's fiscal gap well beyond its current level of $70 trillion.

Benefit Growth and the Fiscal Gap

The fact that the vast majority of Medicare plus Medicaid expenditures goes to the elderly, that average Medicare plus Medicaid payments rise with age, and that the United States is aging all suggest that higher benefit growth could substantially worsen the fiscal gap. Jagadeesh Gokhale's and Kent Smetters's work supports this concern. Their analysis suggests that were Uncle Sam to let benefit levels grow 2 percentage points faster than per capita GDP rather than just 1 percentage point faster (CBO's assumption), the fiscal gap could widen by over $30 trillion.[13] (Recall that the historic average is 2.6 percent faster.) Conversely, limiting benefit growth immediately to the rate of growth of per capita GDP could rid the country of close to half of its fiscal gap. This fact is an eye opener. It and related fiscal gap analyses tell us that projected excessive healthcare growth is the single most important factor in generating our backbreaking fiscal gap.

The Stakes Involved

Let's assume, for the moment, that we make no changes to our current healthcare system and that future growth in Medicare and Medicaid spending accords with the Congressional Budget Office's projections. Under this highly optimistic scenario, the country is, as we know, short today—not tomorrow—$70 trillion.

It's hard to wrap one's brain around $70 trillion. But let's try. The following are four ways to come up with $70 trillion in present value without cutting future growth in Medicare and Medicaid. Each of these policies would need to be implemented immediately and permanently.

- Raise personal and corporate federal income taxes by 70 percent.
- Raise payroll tax rates by 109 percent.
- Cut all federal purchases of goods and service—from buying air force jets to paying the salaries of Supreme Court Justices—by 91 percent.
- Cut social security benefits by 90 percent.

Adopting any one of these policies or some combination would be incredibly painful. But waiting is no alternative. It just makes the requisite adjustments larger and more difficult.

Another option is to implement each of the four policies partially; for example, we could implement each policy at one-fourth strength. But implementing one-fourth of four terribly painful policies still adds up to one terribly painful course of action. The reality is that no American politician would endorse any of these policies or, for that matter, any combination of them that produces $70 trillion in present value.

So what exactly will happen if we don't radically reform the healthcare system and simply let Medicare and Medicaid expenditures continue to grow? The answer is that the government will need to make money by printing it. This practice dates to at least the third century A.D. when the Romans ran a tremendous hyperinflation.

In the twentieth century, twenty countries ran hyperinflations (monthly inflation rates exceeding 20 percent) by printing money to pay their bills. The most famous (or infamous) example is the hyperinflation in the early 1920s in Weimar Germany. Prices rose so fast that workers were paid in wheelbarrows full of cash, which they immediately used to purchase goods so their money wouldn't be worthless by the next day.[14]

The United States is hardly immune to hyperinflation. This is why David M. Walker, comptroller general of the United States, and Ben Bernanke, chairman of the U.S. Federal Reserve, are pulling out their remaining hairs worrying about our long-run fiscal situation.[15] They realize that financial markets can turn on a dime when they start to smell a problem. Doing so in this context means that both foreign and domestic investors would lose confidence in the dollar and attempt to unload their holdings of U.S. securities, particularly long-term U.S. Treasury bonds. This would lead to a crash of both the U.S. bond and stock markets, drive up nominal and real interest rates, and force the Federal Reserve to try to lower interest rates by buying up U.S. bonds. That would require the Fed to create (print) money—precisely what the financial markets will come to fear because they know it fuels inflation.

The point of describing this process is to indicate that when fiscal policy gets sufficiently out of control (the U.S. situation), central banks start to lose control of their monetary independence and are forced to accommodate the inflationary process.

How high would inflation get in the United States? Very high. Most federal government expenditures are explicitly or implicitly indexed to inflation, so to really make money by making (that is, printing) money, the government will have to beat the indexation, which means running ever higher levels of inflation. Running a high inflation, let alone a hyperinflation, would mean dramatic increases in not just nominal but also real interest rates, which would severely damage the economy and its revenue-generating capacity.

I and many other academics, business leaders, and government officials have been sounding this fiscal siren for years. Yet the precipitous crisis we've predicted has not developed. As a result, concern over the fiscal gap appears overblown to many observers.

It's not. Our fiscal problem is real and very serious. The best way to grasp what's going on is to think of a very slowly growing, untreated cancer, which is barely detectable for many years. Then, virtually from one day to the next, it spreads rapidly and alters the functioning of a major organ in a fully perceptible manner. Ex post the cancer is obvious; ex ante no one saw it coming.

Speaking of seeing things coming, how many people saw Argentina's fiscal crisis coming before it hit? How many realized the Russians were in deep trouble in the late 1990s? How many predicted the East Asian crisis or the Mexican peso crisis? And how many foresaw each of the past century's twenty hyperinflations? The answer is not many. And the common factor here is that almost all of these financial and economic collapses were rooted in a tremendous fiscal gap.

The fact that the collapses were missed by most observers is not surprising. It takes a long time to run a well-functioning economy down the tubes. It also takes careful eyes and reliable data to really understand a country's true long-term fiscal position. And it takes international consensus, notoriously slow to form, that an economy is really underwater and can't be rescued by better fiscal policies or improvements in productivity or technology for the alarm to sound.

The best indicator that a country's fiscal policy is out of control and leading an economy to live beyond its means is its national saving rate. Whether the government directly spends an increasing share of a nation's income or arranges its fiscal affairs so that the public does so, the result is higher total consumption relative to national income and a lower ratio of national saving to national income—the national saving rate.

In the U.S. case, it's taken almost five decades of intergenerational redistribution from young savers to old spenders to lower the U.S. national saving rate from its 1960 value of 12.6 percent to its current value of 2.9 percent.[16] And because the United

States is saving so little, we can't keep up with our country's demand for investment. Today's difference between domestic investment and national saving—called the *current account deficit*—is huge. Indeed, for every dollar we Americans are investing in our country, foreigners are investing close to three dollars.

Much of this foreign investment in the United States is in the form of foreigners purchasing claims to U.S. financial assets. For example, the Chinese government now holds upward of $1.3 trillion in U.S. government bonds. Suppose the Chinese were to wake up tomorrow and say, "Gee, we're getting really worried about the U.S. long-term fiscal position. We're getting concerned that the U.S. government will start to print money to pay its bills and cause inflation. We don't want to be sitting here holding claims to worthless dollars. We should sell our U.S. bonds and hold other assets that are more secure."

If the Chinese do pursue this line of thought and decide to sell their U.S. bonds, en masse or even in a significant part, there is no question that it would precipitate a U.S. financial crisis of the first order. There are simply too many bond traders around the world eyeing the Chinese-U.S. bond position nervously for this not to happen.

The Japanese and the Koreans hold lots of U.S. bonds as well. They too could jump ship at any time and tip the boat, if not sink it, in the process. Surely they and the Chinese are aware of the fact that the U.S. dollar has declined relative to the euro by more than 30 percent in recent years. This depreciation of the dollar has, by itself, represented a form of default on their U.S. bond holdings, since these bonds now can only buy roughly 70 percent of the European goods and services they could formerly purchase.

How concerned are world investors about America's fiscal finances? How closely are they examining the huge recent rise in federal discretionary spending? How much does Medicaid's huge expansion matter to their thinking? Are they fully aware of the costs of Medicare Part D? How tired are they getting of holding U.S. securities while the dollar continues to sink?

The answer is we don't know. What we do know is that the United States has been pumping more and more air into an already overinflated tire and that there is a point at which it will burst unless the pressure, particularly in the area of healthcare spending, is released.

3 | Restraining Expenditure Growth: An Anatomy of Failure

The government has tried over the years to limit Medicare and Medicaid expenditure growth using various means. In the case of Medicare, Uncle Sam tried before 1983 to pay Part A (hospital care) providers on "a reasonable cost basis." Since then it's been using the prospective payment system (PPS), which entails classifying each patient as falling into a diagnosis-related group (DRG) and giving the hospital a fixed amount of money for treatment of that DRG. The idea behind the DRG classification is to make the hospital financially responsible, at the margin, for healthcare outlays; that is, since the government's payment per patient is, in theory, fixed, every extra dollar spent by the hospital on the patient means a dollar less in hospital revenue.

Part B (outpatient care) Medicare reimbursements were also originally set on a "reasonable charge" basis. But since 1992, most reimbursements have been made on the basis of a fee schedule. Medicare Part C pays a fixed amount per Medicare participant who enrolls in a health maintenance organization (HMO). And Medicare Part D pays a variable amount based on a preset formula for prescription medications. Medicaid has similar reimbursement methods and is increasingly enrolling participants in HMOs. One big difference between Medicare and Medicaid is that the federal and state governments share Medicaid costs. The federal share differs by state but can range from 50 to 83 percent depending on the state's level of per capita income. The fact that states don't pay, at the margin, the full cost of expanding their Medicaid coverage and benefit levels helps explain why Medicaid spending has grown and continues to grow so rapidly.

In a recent study, Kenneth Thorpe and David Howard, two professors at Emory University's School of Public Health, took a careful look at total Medicare spending growth between 1987 and 2002.[1] They did so by allocating expenditures based on medical conditions. They focused especially on the top ten medical conditions, which, according to their calculations, are associated with two-thirds of the growth in Medicare expenditures over the fifteen-year period.

One of these conditions is heart disease. According to table 3.1, 12.4 percent of the fifteen-year increase in total Medicare spending fell into the heart disease category. A total of 61.3 percent of this 12.4 percent figure can be traced to there simply being more Medicare participants who happened to have heart conditions. Another 33.0 percent of the 12.4 percent arose from higher costs per heart disease case. And the final 5.7 percent share of the 12.4 percent is due to higher prevalence, meaning that any given Medicare enrollee had a higher chance of being treated for heart disease in 2002 than in 1987.

The explanation of the expenditure increases differ from condition to condition. In the case of diabetes, for example, preva-

Table 3.1
Change in health care spending and treated disease prevalence among Medicare beneficiaries for the top ten medical conditions, 1987–2002

	Percent of change in total health care spending associated with the condition, 1987–2002	Percent of change due to		
		Change in prevalence	Change in cost per case	Change in enrollment
Heart Disease	12.39	5.7	33.0	61.3
Mental disorders	9.65	42.3	26.5	31.2
Trauma	7.50	2.9	53.1	44.0
Arthritis	6.83	19.5	38.6	41.8
Hypertension	6.76	13.7	65.6	35.7
Cancer	6.08	35.7	0.8	63.5
Diabetes	5.46	33.9	24.3	41.8
Pulmonary conditions	4.28	42.1	10.9	47.0
Hyperlipidemia	3.36	64.9	7.2	27.9
Cerebrovascular disease	3.40	50.3	4.8	44.9
Total	66.20			

Source: Authors' tabulations based on data from the 1987 and 2002 Medical Expenditure Panel Survey (MEPS), using methods based on S. W. Zuvekas and J. W. Cohen, "A Guide to Comparing Health Care Expenditures in the 1996 MEPS to 1987 NMES," *Inquiry* 39, no. 1 (2002): 76–86.

lence is a much more important factor, explaining a third of the spending increase in that category.

In general, change in prevalence shows up in the table as a major force behind the increased spending. Table 3.2 shows that prevalence rose across all medical conditions. For example, in 1987 there was a 34.8 percent chance that a Medicare beneficiary was treated for hypertension. In 2002 there was a 44.9 percent chance.

The high and rising prevalence rates for so many conditions suggest that Medicare participants typically have more than one condition and that more participants are developing multiple ailments over time. This is exactly the case. According to Thorpe and Howard, 31 percent of participants in 1987 were treated for five or more conditions, with these participants accounting for half of total Medicare spending. In 2002 over half of Medicare participants were treated for five or more conditions, a remarkable increase.

The multiply sick Medicare participants are costing the system big bucks. To quote Thorpe and Howard, "Virtually all of the spending growth since 1987 can be traced to patients treated for five or more conditions." What's going on? Are the elderly getting sicker, or are they simply seeing their doctors more often and being screened for and diagnosed with particular diseases at earlier stages, or are they just being classified in multiple disease/illness categories so that physicians can gain more Medicare reimbursement?

All three factors are at play. One indication that the elderly are indeed experiencing more disease is the size of their waistlines. Back in 1987, fewer than one in ten Medicare beneficiaries were

Table 3.2
Age-adjusted treated disease prevalence among Medicare beneficiaries, 1987, 1997, and 2002

Condition	1987	1997	2002
Hyperlipidemia	2.6%	10.7%	22.2%
Mental disorders	7.9	13.1	19.0
Hyptertension	34.8	37.6	44.9
Osteoporosis and other bone disorders	2.2	5.2	10.3
Pulmonary disorders	15.5	22.0	23.5
Endocrine disorders	14.5	21.4	22.4
Arthritis	21.2	21.5	27.0
Diabetes	11.4	13.7	17.5
Upper GI	6.6	10.3	16.4
Back problems	6.2	8.4	11.3
Other GI	3.4	7.4	7.6
Skin disorders	12.9	14.4	16.8
Lupus	7.7	10.0	11.9
Cancer	10.3	12.5	13.0
Infectious disease	5.3	6.0	6.8
Heart disease	27.0	26.1	27.8
Cerebrovascular disease	2.5	4.6	4.1
Kidney disease	2.2	2.3	3.3
Pneumonia	2.3	3.8	3.4
Trauma	15.8	14.3	16.4

Source: Author's tabulations based on data from the 1987 National Medical Expenditure Survey (NMES) and the 2002 Medical Expenditure Panel Survey (MEPS).
Note: Hyperlipidemia refers to the presence of elevated fatty molecules; GI is gastrointestinal.

obese. Today's figure exceeds two in ten. Clearly, all those super-sized meals are doing real damage. But Thorpe and Howard also point a finger at their doctors for more aggressively treating and, in some cases, overtreating their patients. They report, in this regard, that three of every five Medicare participants with five or more conditions claimed in 2002 to be in either excellent or good health. In 1987 the proportion was only one in three. In addition to seeing doctors for more ailments, patients are seeing their doctors for any given ailment more often, and they are seeing more doctors, particularly specialists, for any given ailment. Moreover, each ailment is being treated over time with a different, and generally more expensive, mix of services—for example, an MRI rather than an X-ray.

In considering this expenditure growth process, the key point to keep front and center is that the government has highly limited control over what it spends. Uncle Sam may say that he'll pay $X and only $X when a doctor sees a patient with condition Y. But the patient is free to see the doctor as often as they both deem appropriate, and the patient is free to see multiple doctors for the same ailment. Any of these doctors can determine that the patient has conditions Q, R, and S as well as Y, and each can prescribe the most expensive testing and treatment plan available.[2]

Many of these behaviors come under the heading "premium medicine," coined by Arnold Kling in *Crisis of Abundance*. Kling defines premium medicine as consisting of (1) frequent referrals to specialists, (2) extensive use of high-tech diagnostic procedures, and (3) increased number and variety of surgeries. Interestingly, the application of premium medicine to the Medicare population seems to be having little if any affect on at least one measure of health, survival rates. Jonathan Skinner and John Wennberg, economists at Dartmouth, report large variations across hospital referral regions in Medicare expenditures per participant in the last six months of life.[3] But they find no evidence that the additional medical care being provided in high expenditure regions is, on average, prolonging life.

I trust you are getting the point: there is no fixed limit on the government's combined Medicare and Medicaid fee-for-service expenditure liability in a given year or over time. Instead, these fee-for-service spending machines are largely on autopilot and will remain that way until we radically change the way the government organizes and pays for healthcare.

Eliminating Fee-for-Service Can Work

Think of a fully open but broken faucet, and you have a vivid picture of fee-for-service spending. There has been a concerted effort in Medicaid to limit fee-for-service by enrolling participants, whether they like it or not, in managed care programs. Back in 1991, only 9.5 percent of Medicaid participants were in managed care. Today's figure is 64.1 percent.[4] This growth in managed care has helped limit growth in real Medicaid benefits per enrollee to only 1.02 percent per year since the early 1990s. The corresponding annual growth rate between 1970 and 1990 was 5.33 percent. Indeed, although it's not well known, real Medicaid benefits per enrollee were actually lower in 2005 than they were in 2000.

Notwithstanding the dramatic decline in the rate of growth of Medicaid benefit levels since 1990, total Medicaid expenditures have continued to explode. The explanation lies in a huge expansion in enrollment in the ensuing years. Medicaid enrollment in 1990 stood at 25.3 million. Today it's north of 60 million. This incredible expansion reflects the increase in the number of uninsured Americans applying for Medicaid and changes in government Medicaid eligibility conditions to permit more Americans to participate. A prime example here is the relatively recent introduction of the State Children's Health Insurance Program (SCHIP), which has brought millions of otherwise uninsured children under Medicaid's umbrella.[5]

The fact that growth in Medicaid benefit levels has been held in check coincident with a policy of states contracting with private HMOs to pay a fixed amount, and no more, to cover their Medicaid participants tells us that moving away from fee-for-service can work.

But to be clear, what's special in the Medicaid case is that the government has a degree of coercive power in dealing with the poor that it doesn't have in dealing with the general population, particularly the elderly. The government, in the form of state Medicaid officials, can tell Medicaid participants, "You're in this HMO, like it or not. And whatever the plan covers, that's the maximum you'll get." Also, the states are free to enroll all of their Medicaid participants in a single HMO. This is critically important: it means they can act like a large employer that can get a group rate because the HMO can be relatively assured of the healthcare status of the entire pool of participants. Were the states instead to tell their participants, "Please choose among whatever HMO you'd like," the HMOs would need to worry about adverse selection—the propensity of those with the greatest risks to seek the most insurance coverage. They'd also have to

worry about other HMOs establishing features of their own services, such as free gym privileges, that were designed to attract
and thus siphon off the healthiest Medicaid participants and
leave the remaining HMOs with the least healthy to insure.

Medicare—You Can't Get to Medicaid from Here

Could Medicare participants be treated in the same way as
Medicaid participants? In theory, yes. In practice, no. Most
Medicare participants are elderly and either middle class or rich.
Most are used to getting their way in life, and most vote with
great regularity. Politicians know this and live in mortal fear
that they will even mildly perturb the powerful oldsters' lobby
group—the AARP (formerly called the American Association of
Retired Persons).

Consequently, Uncle Sam has never forced Medicare participants to join HMOs. Instead, Uncle Sam has left the choice up to
Medicare participants as to whether they'd like to join an HMO.
The notion was that HMOs would have every incentive to limit
unnecessary medical care because, at the margin, they'd have to
pay for it. The hope was that HMOs would introduce enough
competition into the medical sector that Medicare would also
save money on participants who remained in the traditional fee-
for-service program.

Things didn't work out as expected. The HMOs realized what
Congress was up to and sought out the healthiest Medicare
participants. At the same time, the least healthy Medicare participants realized that joining HMOs would mean facing restric-
tions, such as less access to second opinions and to specialists,
on their level of care, so they stayed away. The result was that

the government overpaid many HMOs for taking on the relatively healthy and inexpensive Medicare beneficiaries who actually signed up.

In the case of HMOs that inadvertently found themselves with particularly sick and expensive Medicare beneficiaries, the solution was simple: ask the government for more money. When the government refused, these HMOs simply kicked out their existing Medicare patients and stopped taking on new ones. In recent years, half of the HMO programs established by private companies to enroll Medicare participants have closed. In so doing, they simply told 1.1 million Medicare beneficiaries to get lost. In short, giving Medicare participants discretion in choosing whether to join HMOs encouraged adverse selection, with the good risks joining the HMOs and the bad risks remaining in traditional Medicare. And since the payments to the HMOs made by Medicare were based on the average cost of *all* participants (those not enrolling in HMOs as well as those enrolling), Medicare ended up overpaying the HMOs to cover the participants who signed up, thereby costing, rather than saving, the system money. If repeating the successes of Medicaid in limiting Medicare benefit growth is not possible, what is? The answer is a system of universal health insurance: healthcare coverage that explicitly limits government payments at the margin, permits consumer choice, and overcomes adverse selection. Before presenting this proposed new system, I'm going to ask: Why it is that government is in this business in the first place? The answer is not simply the ability and apparent desire of self-interested oldsters to extract resources from youngsters. Nor is it simply that adverse selection makes a hash of the private health insurance market. The answer also involves paternalism.

4   The Imperatives of Paternalism

I'm a paternalist. I favor a certain amount of government intervention to limit the damage we can do to ourselves and to others. I believe, for example, that parents should be forced to have their children vaccinated. But I don't want to argue the pros and cons of paternalism in general or to defend my own brand of paternalism. Rather, I want to point out that virtually all Americans, no matter what their political affiliation, religious orientation, or ethnic background, subscribe to a common set of paternalistic desiderata that I call the *Principles of American Paternalism*. Once we collectively and clearly acknowledge this fact and examine where our paternalism begins and ends, it's a pretty straightforward matter to design health insurance and other social insurance programs that satisfy our paternalistic principles at least cost, are generationally equitable, and take full account of the adverse selection problem. As things now stand, we have a set of paternalistic policies, most notably healthcare policies, that don't work. And they don't work in large part because of the desire of certain segments of society to disguise their paternalism for fear of being labeled a liberal, a socialist, a

Democrat, an advocate of big government, or something else of that nature.

Worrying about how we sound rather than what we are doing has kept us from enunciating and, thereby, hearing and perceiving, our shared beliefs. An example is providing healthcare to the uninsured. The fact of the matter is that our country—right here and right now—has universal healthcare: everyone, even the uninsured, gets healthcare in this country. Those who are really sick can walk into most emergency rooms in the country's hospitals and receive care regardless of whether they can pay for it. (They may get stuck with a big credit card bill, but they'll be seen and treated.)

The reason that we effectively have universal healthcare is that almost all Americans feel that someone who is sick and needs to be treated by a doctor must, in the end, be so treated even if he or she can't pay for the treatment. Whether one wants to call healthcare a right or use some other word is irrelevant to the basic fact that we are securing this outcome for all Americans, albeit in one of the most inefficient and inhumane ways possible.

Who picks up the tab for those who aren't packing credit cards when they show up at the emergency room and can't pay their ER bills? The hospitals. And who supports the hospitals? Federal, state, or local government. It may be that a local hospital receives support from local authorities, which in turn receive support from state authorities, which in turn receive support from federal authorities. This support can be of a general nature or earmarked toward healthcare. It doesn't matter. A dollar's a dollar.

By setting things up so that the hospitals appear to be covering, out of the goodness of their institutional hearts, those uninsured who either can't or won't pay, we try to cover up the fact that it is the government that's really paying these bills. This lets us pretend that this part of our healthcare system is private, when it's actually best characterized as a combined public-private system.

The mixed public-private nature of our nation's healthcare system is, in fact, ubiquitous. There is no element of our current system that doesn't incorporate significant public as well as private components. Employer-provided health insurance is a case in point. The fact that employer-based health insurance premiums are not taxable represents an enormous public subsidy. Indeed, one can just as well say that what's going on is that the workers covered by these policies receive no tax break, but the government directly pays part of the workers' insurance premiums.

Our current public-private healthcare system is incredibly expensive, inefficient, and exceptionally financially hazardous to maintain. The U.S. level of per capita healthcare spending is the highest in the world; indeed, it's roughly twice that of the typical developed country. Yet consider any indicator of healthcare efficacy—infant mortality rates, morbidity rates, longevity—and the United States ranks with developing countries. Moreover, a variety of studies point to administrative costs that absorb an incredibly high fraction of each U.S. healthcare dollar. An article in the *New England Journal of Medicine*, for example, shows that 31 percent of every healthcare dollar spent in the United States goes to administration compared with 17 percent in Canada.[1]

The bang from our healthcare buck is remarkably small. We're paying a huge price for packaging our healthcare delivery in ways that permit closet paternalists to pretend they aren't giving away healthcare for free.

Paternalism—Left, Right, and Center

Socialism is the boogeyman of libertarians and many Republicans, and for good reason. They connect the word *socialism* with Soviet-style collectivization, which represented the ultimate form of state control and trampled the rights and liberties of hundreds of millions of people for much of the previous century. *State power, state control, state intervention, state regulation*: the very recitation of these words makes a true libertarian's blood boil.

What makes the true libertarian smile is the thought of restraining the state, limiting its power, keeping it at bay, and circumscribing its influence. Eliminating all centralization of power is the ultimate dream of a true libertarian. The name of the nation's leading libertarian think tank—the Cato Institute—was not chosen by accident: Cato was the Roman senator who chose suicide over submission to Julius Caesar's dictatorship.

Given their visceral reaction to anything that smacks of socialism, libertarians and others who share their concerns often have a hard time acknowledging that they are paternalistic. Being paternalistic, after all, means you know what's best for someone else and are prepared to make sure that what you know is best for that person actually happens. Examples are forcing children to go to school, requiring parents to seek medical care for their children, and making people save for their retirement.

No self-respecting libertarian is likely to proclaim his or her paternalism. You won't hear the Cato Institute publicly deny anyone the right to lay down sick in the gutter and die. Instead, the organization's macho creed is that people should look after themselves and that no one should be forced to help anyone else unless he or she really wants to do so. This "let them eat cake" mantra works just fine for fund raising, but when it comes to setting policies that would let children and others suffer from a curable disease or let people starve, the Cato Institute sings a different tune.

Part of this may be simply bowing to political reality, but I think there is a deeper explanation. At the core of a libertarian's belief system is that each of us is his own person and that what someone else does to himself and what happens to someone else is that person's own business and no one else's. That proposition works fine except for the fact that almost all of us care about other people. We aren't simply self-interested. We are, at least to some degree, altruistic. And this caring for others means that when someone else hurts himself or allows himself to get hurt, that person is doing real damage not just to himself but also to us.

The fact that libertarians, no matter their pretensions, also feel other people's pain means that they too have a personal interest in compelling and controlling other people's behavior and outcomes. Thus, it should be no real surprise that if you look closely at what the Cato Institute advocates, it often entails a fair amount of paternalism. Take social security reform. Cato doesn't advocate abolishing compulsory saving. Instead, it implicitly accepts the need to force people to save, but wants people to be able to choose their investments.[2]

Members of the Cato Institute are far from the only closet paternalists around. One can make the case that the Republican party is now and has long been a bastion of paternalism. George W. Bush and the 2004 Republican Congress were, after all, the architects of the most recent and one of the most expensive paternalistic policies ever adopted in the United States. I speak, of course, of Medicare Part D, which assures low-income households that they will no longer need to choose between heating oil, cat food, and medicine by effectively bribing the elderly to acquire government-provided prescription-drug insurance coverage.

Moving farther back in time, we find that both Presidents Eisenhower and Nixon dramatically expanded the scale of social security, that President Nixon introduced Supplemental Security Income and expanded Medicaid, that Presidents Reagan and Bush I expanded Medicaid, and that the 1997 Republican Congress established SCHIP, which provides health coverage to low-income children who don't qualify for Medicaid. Tellingly, Senator Orrin G. Hatch, the noted conservative Republican senator from Utah, was the author of SCHIP, together with none other than Senator Edward Kennedy, arguably the nation's most liberal senator.

Yet another example of Republican paternalism is the initiatives undertaken in 2006 by Massachusetts governor Mitt Romney and in 2007 by California governor Arnold Schwarzenegger, both staunch Republicans, to compel universal healthcare for all of their state's citizens. Many other states around the nation with either Republican governors or legislatures are also considering mandating universal health insurance coverage.

Politicians are, of course, strongly guided by public opinion. In the case of universal healthcare, opinion is heavily in favor of the introduction of such a system. Indeed, a 2005 Pew poll determined that two-thirds of Americans support universal healthcare even at the cost of higher taxes. Among self-described "social conservatives," support was almost as strong: 59 percent.[3]

To be sure, much of the support for universal healthcare is coming from the 47 million uninsured, and much is coming from the millions of insured who see the prospects of losing their own coverage and even their jobs because of escalating healthcare costs. But my sense is that the vast majority of Americans would endorse the following ten fundamental principles of paternalism even were their own healthcare and jobs fully secure:

Principles of American Paternalism
1. No American should go without food and water.
2. No American should go without shelter.
3. No American should go without clothing.
4. No American should go without sanitary facilities.
5. No American should go without physical protection.
6. No American should go without legal representation.
7. No American should go without equal opportunity.
8. No child should go without education.
9. No child should go without vaccination.
10. No American should go without basic medical care.

Self-inspection is a good way to check if the nation supports these principles. If our country has policies in place that uphold these principles, we can safely conclude that they have broad support. I refer to this as *revealed societal paternalism* and want to ask whether our country does in fact support these principles in deed as well as discourse.

Consider principles 1 through 4. Although one can argue that America's soup kitchens, homeless shelters, Goodwill stores, food drives, religious charities, food stamps program, Transitional Aid to Families with Dependent Children program, Women Infants Children program, Low Income Housing Energy Assistance Program, Supplemental Security Income program, Department of Housing and Urban Development shelter and low-income housing assistance programs, and similar private and public initiatives, institutions, and policies could be better funded and organized, they do seem to reflect strong support for the first four principles. Next think about principles 5, 6, and 7. They are fundamental features of our civil justice system. The poorest and weakest members of society can call 911 for police protection, obtain a public defender if they are subject to criminal prosecution, and obtain redress in the courts against employment discrimination.

As for principles 8 and 9, every public school district in the country makes sure these two principles are enforced.

This leaves principle 10, which I'd like to consider bit by bit since the definition of "basic medical care" is up for grabs. Let's start with emergency medical care. It's obvious that such care is available to everyone. No matter who you are or where you live, you can call 911 for emergency medical assistance and expect paramedics to rush to your side. You may be penniless and have no prospect of securing future income. Yet the ambulance will come when called and find a hospital to fix your broken leg, treat your heart attack, dress your burns, or whatever else is needed. And no one will ask for your credit card prior to administering CPR.

The story is no different if instead of calling an ambulance, you drag yourself into the emergency room. You may be pressed for payment information or a payment method, but you will almost always be seen and given proper medical treatment, even if you are dirt poor and can't pay for the treatment.

Next, consider more routine outpatient care as well as scheduled tests and operations at hospitals. To get this care, you will be pressed for a payment method. But many clinics, hospitals, and doctors will provide assistance for little or no compensation if you have no way to pay. And if you do have a payment means but are forced to use up your assets and income in the process of paying for your healthcare, the medical establishment won't terminate your treatment just because you've run out of resources. Indeed, once you have dissipated your resources, the government will step in, enroll you in Medicaid, and pay your medical bills through that program.

The point is that principle 10 is satisfied in the United States, albeit not without putting a lot of low- and middle-income people through the ringer and into the poorhouse. So why is that? Why is it that we want everyone to have good medical care but don't want them to get it for free if they can afford to pay for it? The answer is that we don't want others to free-ride on our generosity—to take advantage of us and make us pay for something they should buy for themselves.

Economists call this problem the Samaritan's dilemma.[4] The title derives from Jesus's story about the Good Samaritan in which a good person Y takes care of a poor person X. Clearly Y cares about X, and this caring underlies Y's paternalistic actions. Jesus says that Y should love X and that X should love Y, and I should love you and you should love me, and that we should all be one big loving family and automatically take care of each other. But what Jesus omits is that in helping X, Y has to worry that X will take advantage of his caring and press him for more help in the future. This is Y's dilemma—the Samaritan's dilemma.

Jesus was no economist. Had he been one, he might have had Y tell X, "You know, X, I'd really like to help you, but I'm worried you'll take advantage of me. Furthermore, we might be in opposite shoes tomorrow, in which case if you were to help me, I'd be tempted thereafter to take advantage of you. So let's do the following: let's get Uncle Sam to force both of us to work, save, and insure so that we can both take care of ourselves and neither can free-ride on the other."

This is the simple solution. It explains why we established the social security and Medicare systems. In so doing, we effectively forced ourselves to save, buy life insurance, and buy old age health insurance. Come again? Well, when we pay payroll taxes, we secure claims to social security retirement and survivor benefits, as well as to future Medicare benefits.[5] Yes, any given contributor may not get back, on an actuarial basis, what she contributes; there is certainly massive redistribution across and within generations associated with these programs. But that doesn't negate the fact that these policies to a large extent compel provision for one's own future.

Mind you, we could arrange things differently. We could leave people to save, buy life insurance, and buy old age health insurance completely on their own and then provide it for them if they failed to do so and extract some awful penalty if they failed to comply. Were we to do this, we'd have treatment roughly parallel to how we provide universal healthcare. Recall that we most certainly do provide universal healthcare in this country. We just do so in a way that leaves many low-income (but not super-low-income) and middle-class workers facing an awful penalty—huge financial losses, potentially including bankruptcy if they fail to buy their own preretirement health insurance and wind up needing extensive medical care.

Why have we arranged things to take good care of the elderly but not the working population? Is there something intrinsically different about our paternalism with respect to people's health when they are young and old? I don't think so. I don't think we feel less bad about seeing a thirty-year-old suffer from a curable medical condition than a seventy-year-old suffering from the same condition.

What is different is that, at least in the past, a thirty-year-old had a pretty good chance of receiving health insurance coverage on the job. And thirty-year-olds who didn't were able in the past to purchase reasonably priced private health insurance to avoid financial ruin from gallbladder surgery or some other relatively expensive, unexpected medical problem.

Today employers are busy getting out of the health insurance business. Moreover, buying health insurance as an individual has become prohibitively expensive. We need a new solution to healthcare paternalism as it applies to children, young adults, and the middle-aged who are not covered by Medicaid and are not rich enough to self-insure.

As with the case of guaranteeing that our fellow compatriots have enough to live on in old age, receive medical care in old age, and provide for their dependents if they die before reaching old age, there is a solution that avoids the Samaritan's dilemma. The solution is compulsion: force people to purchase their health insurance for themselves and their children when they are young just like we force them to purchase assets (future social security retirement and dependent benefits), life insurance (social security survivor benefits), and old age health insurance (Medicare benefits) when they are young.

In the latter three cases, the forcing comes in the form of having to pay FICA as well as federal income and other taxes. And yes, I realize that there is no strict accounting that connects what one person pays when young and receives when old. Money is fungible, and there is no way that anyone can prove he or she is paying for his or her own future benefits with specific taxes. This point has a corollary: there is also no way to disprove such a proposition.

But set this argument aside. The main point is that we are all compelled to pay taxes and we are all endowed with (provided entitlement to) these three types of benefits.

If you've followed my drift, you'll know that I'm advocating more of what works. I'm for compelling both X and Y to purchase medical insurance when they are young so that X (Y) doesn't need to help pay Y's (X's) medical bills if Y (X) gets sick.

There are lots of ways to compel payment for medical insurance, but the most efficient way is to use the tax system. The reason is that the government can garner workers' wages before they are potentially dissipated on a variety of purchases that don't include health insurance premiums.

Of course, having the government collect all the money for health insurance premiums also means that the government would be paying out this money to cover the relevant population with medical goods and services. This starts sounding like the government would directly provide the medical goods and services for the entire population, which starts to sound like European, Japanese, and Canadian healthcare systems.

This is not the case.

Collecting the money that ultimately will pay for medical goods and services doesn't mean providing those goods and services directly. The structure of Medicare and Medicaid as it now stands makes that clear. Uncle Sam and Aunt Sally (she runs state government) don't directly buy the pills and hire the doctors and train the nurses and build the hospitals that treat the Medicare and Medicaid populations. They just pay the providers. But it is the providers and their patients who jointly determine the nature and extent of medical expenditures. The fact that this method of determining what gets spent is designed to be extraordinarily expensive and inefficient (particularly in the case of Medicare) is true, but that's besides this particular point.

My solution, the Medical Security System (MSS), which I'll present shortly, would achieve our paternalistic objectives in the area of healthcare without having the government micromanage the delivery of care. It would implement universal health insurance, not universal healthcare.

Of course, the MSS would need to be paid for. But as we'll see, the government is already collecting enough taxes to cover the vast majority of the expenses associated with implementing the MSS. This fact alleviates not just the concern about how to pay for MSS, but also the worry that in going to universal health insurance, governments would need to enact much higher taxes and that these much higher taxes would significantly undermine incentives to work and save.

Adverse Selection: The Bugaboo of Healthcare Reform

In compelling everyone through their collective tax contributions to purchase health insurance, the MSS plan recognizes and deals with the biggest problem facing private insurance companies in the healthcare arena: the fact that they don't know who they are dealing with. This is less of a problem when insurance companies are insuring a large number of workers of a major company. These workers will, as a group, be close to the average when it comes to their ultimate healthcare costs.

But when insurance companies, no matter how large, are asked by someone off the street for an insurance policy quote—someone who may know, but not reveal, that, for example, she has a family history of breast cancer—insurers get mighty nervous. Their response is to set very high insurance premiums to make sure they don't get stuck insuring someone with a high probability of major medical expenses.

Economists refer to the tendency of bad (adverse) risks to demand (select) higher levels of insurance coverage as adverse selection. The adverse selection problem plagues most insurance markets and can often effectively prevent the marketing of insurance to the general public by the private market. If insurance companies need to protect themselves from bad risks by setting super-high premiums, then only the bad risks will be willing to buy the insurance, leaving all the regular and good risks uninsured. This is called a lemons market because only the bad risks (the lemons) are left in the market.

One glance at today's private insurance market, which has left 47 million people out in the cold, shows that adverse selection is strongly at play and has effectively destroyed the nonemployer-based private health insurance market. Any government policy that encourages or compels the public to purchase a healthcare insurance policy from a private insurance carrier must recognize this paramount problem of adverse selection. Specifically, if the government gives every citizen the same amount of money to purchase a policy, the insurance companies will naturally try to figure out who are the good and bad risks and choose to insure the good risks and turn away the bad.

The way around this is to recognize that the heart of the adverse selection problem is asymmetry in information: potential insurees know more about their medical conditions than the insurers do. The government needs to (1) make this information available to insurers and (2) compensate those insurers facing higher expected costs for covering individuals with known health problems. Doing both 1 and 2 will give the insurance companies the incentive to cover the bad as well as the good risks. The reason is that the bad risks will now be able and willing to pay higher premiums in the light of their higher expected costs. This is the essence of my MSS proposal. But before presenting this plan, let me examine what others have proposed with respect to providing health insurance to the uninsured. Let's start with the president's proposal.

I argued in chapter 4 that paternalism is at the heart of why we are concerned not just about our own but also about everyone else's healthcare. I've also claimed that the Samaritan's dilemma naturally leads paternalists (including libertarian paternalists) to compel individuals to provide for their own healthcare. And I've pointed out that those who are devising a plan that entails private insurance companies' marketing of health insurance policies to the general public must directly confront the adverse selection problem if the plan is to be successful. So in considering alternative schemes for expanding health insurance coverage, bear in mind these three requirements:

- Insurance coverage must be universal.
- Insurance coverage must be compulsory.
- Insurance coverage must be affordable even for those with pre-existing conditions or medically suspect family histories.

The Bush Plan

In his January 23, 2007, State of the Union address, President Bush said "We will strengthen health savings accounts, making sure individuals and small-business employees can buy insurance with the same advantages that people working for big businesses now get." According to the president's plan, all married (single) workers would be able to deduct up to $15,000 ($7,500) in annual health insurance premium payments or health saving account contributions from their taxes. This policy would replace the current tax treatment that allows employers to treat premiums they pay for their group plans as an employment expense, but not include those payments on their workers' W2 forms as part of their taxable compensation. Consequently, employees who are covered by employer health insurance plans don't have to pay income or payroll taxes on that part of their compensation that goes to purchase health insurance on their behalf.

For workers now covered by an employer plan, there would be no change in tax treatment provided the current premiums paid by employers on their behalf do not exceed $15,000. If they do exceed $15,000, the difference would become taxable income to the worker. Apparently some 20 percent of workers have plans that entail more than $15,000 in annual premium payments, and these workers would see their taxes rise.

The president's proposal would effectively remove employers from deciding how much one pays in taxes, at least in the healthcare arena. In this regard, the president's plan is long overdue. But as a scheme to expand health insurance coverage, his plan has four fatal flaws.

First, there is no compulsion. No one is compelled under the president's plan to purchase health insurance. This means everyone is free to remain uninsured and thereby free-ride on everyone else's altruism. Second, there is nothing in the president's plan that deals with adverse selection. True, the plan permits states to experiment with different mechanisms to subsidize insurance purchase, but there is no suggestion of a role for the federal government in experience rating (assessing expected healthcare costs of) individual Americans and compensating those with preexisting conditions for their higher expected costs.

Third, the proposal treats premium payments as tax deductible rather than as a refundable tax credit. Consequently, low-income households that don't pay income taxes or whose income taxes are very small won't receive any help or very much help in purchasing health insurance. These households are currently the least likely to purchase health insurance.

Fourth, since higher-income households are in higher tax brackets, the president's plan, although it caps the subsidy on health insurance premiums, still provides a higher subsidy rate (up to the ceiling) for the rich than for the poor.

The president's healthcare plan is not the first time he has proposed something that won't work. Early in his first administration, he proposed, and Congress enacted, legislation establishing health savings accounts (HSAs). These accounts let people save up on their own for their future health bills on an after-tax basis provided they purchase a high-deductible health insurance policy.

Some 3 million Americans may ultimately end up choosing HSAs. That's the good news. The bad news is that HSAs suffer from the same four shortcomings as the president's latest initiative. In addition, they leave their participants exposed to significant medical expense risk since insurance protection kicks in only after a relatively high deductible has been satisfied. One of the goals of implementing HSAs was to extend the tax breaks afforded to employees of firms providing health insurance to those not so covered. But HSA's catch—that those covered need to remain fully exposed to small and moderate health insurance expenditure risks—hardly makes it a level playing field with respect to employer-provided plans.

The reason the Bush administration has been so keen to ensure that health insurance not include too much insurance is the view that when people have to pay, at the margin, on their own (out of their own pockets), they will limit what they spend on healthcare. In general Americans pay only fourteen cents of each additional dollar spent on healthcare thanks to Medicare, Medicaid, and private insurers. And because no one has much incentive to keep track of all this spending, medical goods and services prices have been rising like crazy. The one area of medicine where prices have actually declined in real terms is cosmetic surgery, which is covered neither by government healthcare programs nor by private health insurance.[1] Between 1992 and 2005, the price rises of all medical goods and services averaged 77 percent, whereas the consumer price index rose by 39 percent. Cosmetic surgery prices, on the other hand, went up by only 22 percent.

There is, of course, nothing to stop employers from designing their health insurance compensation to make their workers pay high or even super-high deductibles. The fact that they haven't done so strongly suggests that workers desire full or very close to full coverage.

This brings me to the fourth major problem with the president's latest initiative: the ongoing marginal subsidization of health insurance. As with the existing primarily employer-based health insurance system, the president's plan continues to use the tax system to subsidize the purchase of health insurance. It does so by maintaining the deductibility of contributions, at least up to the $15,000 ceiling. This means that for typical households, it costs less to buy a dollar of health insurance coverage than it does to buy a dollar of other goods and services because every dollar spent on health insurance premiums entails a tax break equal to the dollar multiplied by the household's marginal tax rate.

This is surely one of the key reasons that private sector health expenditures have been rising so rapidly. Take someone earning below the payroll tax ceiling who is in the 28 percent federal income tax bracket and 5 percent state income tax bracket. Each dollar spent on health insurance premiums saves 28 cents in income taxes plus 5 cents in state income taxes plus 15 cents in payroll taxes; so a dollar's expenditure on health insurance premiums costs only 52 cents on net. The MSS proposal has none of this. It entails no subsidy at the margin with respect to the purchase of extra health insurance.

Hillary Care

In 1993 the Clinton administration proposed an elaborate plan to mandate that all Americans not in Medicare purchase health insurance coverage through HMOs. The scheme has been dubbed "Hillary Care" because it was developed by a task force chaired by then First Lady Hillary Rodham Clinton. The proposed legislation was entitled the Health Security Act.[2] The plan would have formed large participant groups on a region-specific basis to pool risks. Insurers providing coverage to anyone in the pool would have been required to cover everyone else in the pool who also requested coverage.

Members of a particular pool would have been free to select their own HMO. The government would have limited growth in the premium payments exacted by the HMOs. Each participating HMO would have been required to provide a minimum set of benefits (coverages). Each participant would have made different copayments and faced different deductibles depending on his or her choice of an HMO plan. Regional and corporate health alliances would have organized the health pool groups and contracted with HMOs. Corporate alliances would have been made up of firms with 5,000 or more employees. All employers would have been forced to contribute on behalf of their employees to their employees' health alliance. Individuals who were not employed would have been forced to contribute to their alliance on their own, subject to government income-based subsidies. The government would have experience-rated each alliance and redistributed income among them.

Hillary Care, for all its bad press, had a number of sensible features. First, it compelled participation and provided universal coverage. Second, it dealt with adverse selection using cross-alliance experience rating. Third, it ensured that those with preexisting conditions or bad family health histories were not subject to discrimination. Fourth, it permitted some flexibility in the design of insurance copayments, deductibles, and related financial arrangements, thereby permitting the introduction of incentives to limit overuse of the healthcare system.

Notwithstanding these pluses, the system would have required a huge bureaucracy to implement and was exceedingly hard for the public to grasp. Finally, Hillary Care would have done nothing to rein in runaway expenditures on Medicare since it exempted Medicare participants entirely from the program.

The Massachusetts and California Mandatory Health Insurance Plans

In April 2006 former Republican governor Mitt Romney of Massachusetts signed a law mandating that all Massachusetts employers with ten or more employees pay $300 annually per otherwise uninsured employee to assist in the purchase for them of health insurance coverage. The new law also created the Commonwealth Health Insurance Connector to direct the uninsured to quality insurance products. And it called for the state to heavily subsidize premium payments for low-income households. The state also indicated it would significantly expand its enrollment within Medicaid of otherwise uninsured children. Finally, the state indicated that it intended to pay for a basic plan for the uninsured from its own general revenues, Medicaid funds, and the annual $300 employer premium payments. Recently, however, the state has indicated that it may need to pare down the coverage provided by the basic plan owing to higher-than-expected costs. Moreover, the Bush administration has told Massachusetts and other states that it's not willing to approve their planned expansions of the SCHIP portion of Medicaid.

Governor Schwarzenegger's mandatory health insurance plan for Californians is also short of cash. The governor is proposing taxing doctors and hospitals to come up with revenue to pay doctors and hospitals. Like robbing Peter to pay Peter. Employers who aren't currently providing health insurance for their workers would be required to pay a 4 percent payroll tax for that purpose. Like Massachusetts, the California plan seeks to expand Medicaid to cover many of its currently uninsured children. In addition, all individuals would be required by law to purchase a policy with a minimum benefit if they were not already covered. Low-income individuals would be eligible for a generous state subsidy that would help them purchase this plan. Finally, the governor proposed a reward system, such as subsidized gym membership, for those who participate in public health programs, including, no doubt, body building.

The Massachusetts and California plans would provide some health insurance coverage for the uninsured. But both do so by relying on a significant expansion of their Medicaid populations and the receipt of additional federal assistance. As such, they will exacerbate the federal government health financing problem were the federal government to comply. In addition, rather than get employers out of the health insurance business, the Massachusetts and California plans effectively lock them into it.

In mandating employer payments for health insurance, these plans could have some very negative repercussions. Employers who might otherwise be willing to maintain health insurance coverage for their new employees may worry that they'll lose the ability to cut back on health insurance coverage for new employees in the future. Consequently, they may choose to freeze their existing health insurance plans to cover only existing employees and announce that they will contribute the state-specified and state-sanctified minimum for each new employee.

Another concern is finding insurance carriers willing to insure at a rock-bottom price populations that will almost surely have much worse health outcomes than those of the general public. Inducing these carriers to provide health insurance to these segments of society will surely require highly complex experience-rating mechanisms of precisely the same nature as those that made Hillary Care look like a bureaucratic nightmare.

Both Massachusetts and California require that everyone who does not receive health insurance on the job purchase health insurance privately. But telling the otherwise uninsured that they must buy insurance and enforcing such a statement are two different things. No state is going to lock someone up if they fail to buy a health insurance policy. Indeed, Massachusetts is just rolling out its plan, but has already signaled it would exempt some 60,000 state residents from the requirement.[3]

There are other national and state plans, including those of the presidential candidates, for covering the uninsured, but all seem to be variants on those just discussed. There is, however, one notable exception: universal healthcare vouchers, a proposal by Ezekiel Emanuel of the National Institutes of Health and Stanford economics professor Victor Fuchs. This plan, which is similar in many ways to MSS, would provide each American with a government certificate entitling them to join a health plan of their choice, whose cost would be borne fully by the government.[4] Apparently other economists have been thinking for some time about a health insurance voucher.[5] According to Princeton health economist Uwe Reinhart, the idea was first proposed in 1971 by Paul M. Ellwood, viewed by many as the father of managed competition among private insurance carriers.[6] It was subsequently proposed in the early 1970s by Herman and Anne Somers, two Princeton economists. I first heard of the idea of providing individually experience-rated health insurance vouchers from John Goodman, director of the National Center for Policy Analysis. Goodman, as I understand it, worked on the idea in the 1990s with economist Peter Ferrara.[7]

It's time to face facts. Our government is going broke paying for healthcare. So are many of our top companies, and so are millions of individual American households. It's time to take a radical approach to fixing healthcare in America before it fixes us.

The root of the Medicare spending-growth problem is the program's fee-for-service structure: healthcare providers can charge Medicare a fee when they provide Medicare participants a service. One might think that capping the fees would limit total expenditures, but doctors and hospitals can simply change the classifications of the services they provide to ones that provide higher fees. Or they schedule more visits. Or they order more expensive tests and procedures. Or they do all of the above.

As if growth in benefit levels didn't generate enough overall spending growth, the government has deemed it necessary over time to expand what's covered by Medicare, with prescription drugs being the latest and most expensive addition to the list. According to columnist George Will, it represents "the largest expansion of the welfare state since the Great Society 40 years ago."[1] Increased enrollment has been another huge driver of Medicare costs. Population growth of the elderly plus the extension of Medicare coverage to the disabled in the early 1970s have been the major factors in this regard.

There is every reason for Medicare costs to continue to explode and threaten our nation's finances and our children's economic futures. Fee for service remains the predominant payment mechanism for Medicare and is likely to permit benefit growth in excess of per capita income growth as far as the eye can see. Even under recklessly optimistic assumptions in which the excess Medicare benefit growth rate in the future is only two-fifths of its historic value, the nation faces a Medicare bill it cannot afford.

Medicaid has achieved some success in recent years in limiting the growth in the level of real benefits per beneficiary. It has done so by enrolling the majority of its participants in HMOs under fixed-price contracts. But because of the meltdown in private sector insurance arrangements and the induced broadening of eligibility rules, the Medicaid participant population has boomed. Many state governments now intend to enroll millions of more children in the program as part of their plans to achieve universal health insurance coverage.[2]

The problems with private sector health insurance should come as no surprise. For decades the government has strongly encouraged growth in private healthcare spending by using the tax system to subsidize healthcare. This is particularly the case for high-income workers with employer-provided health insurance. For such workers, every dollar spent on healthcare costs roughly 50 to 65 cents on an after-tax basis.

The government-induced healthcare spending spree in conjunction with rising incomes among high-skilled workers has led to much better and much more expensive procedures, treatments, and medications. Rather than restrict the use of these new medical goods and services, and thereby risk being sued, health insurers have passed on their costs in terms of higher premiums. In the process, health insurers are increasingly pricing low-skilled workers and firms hiring such workers out of the market. In addition, the increasing prevalence of disease among the American population, stemming to a significant degree from our collective addiction to junk food and its associated consequences—incredible rates of obesity, with its attendant diabetes, cardiovascular, and other problems—has exacerbated the ever prevalent insurance market bogeyman: adverse selection.[3]

Getting Real

There is no way that we can maintain Medicare's fee-for-service method of paying the medical bills of the elderly. There is also no way we can let 47 million Americans, 8 million of them children, continue to be exposed to devastating financial risk because they or their parents can't afford or don't choose to buy health insurance. Nor can we fix this problem by letting the uninsured impoverish themselves to the point that their incomes and assets are so low that they can qualify for Medicaid.

The Medical Security System I propose (see box) offers a solution that satisfies our paternalistic imperatives as well as our individual and collective pocketbooks. Its ten provisions follow and are repeated on the last page of the book, which may be cut out and mailed to your congressperson.

The Medical Security System

1. Provides universal coverage.

2. Offers each American, annually, a health plan voucher.

3. Those with higher expected healthcare costs receive bigger vouchers.

4. Participants can change their health plans annually.

5. Government defines basic policy each year.

6. Basic policy covers drugs, home healthcare, and nursing home care.

7. Plans must cover basic policy.

8. Plans compete for participants.

9. Annual voucher budget is fixed as share of GDP.

10. Medicare, Medicaid, and employer-based health insurance tax breaks are eliminated.

How MSS Would Work

MSS participants would receive a voucher each year, on October 1, to use to purchase insurance coverage (a health plan, including, but not restricted to HMOs) for the following calendar year. By January 1 of each year, everyone would be signed up with an insurance provider for the year.

The size of the annual voucher would be based on the participant's current medical condition. Hence, a perfectly healthy sixty-seven-year-old might get a voucher for $8,000, whereas an eighty-five-year-old with diabetes might get a voucher for $80,000. Because those in the worst medical shape would have the largest vouchers, insurance carriers would be just as happy to have them as customers as their healthy contemporaries.

Once a participant signs up with an insurance company or HMO, that organization would pay all medical bills incurred over the course of the year. If the initially healthy sixty-seven-year-old has a heart attack during the year and requires $28,000 in care, the insurer or HMO will lose $20,000 on that customer. If the eighty-five-year-old with diabetes ends up requiring only $20,000 in care, the insurer or HMO will earn $60,000 on that customer.

The government would determine the size of each participant's voucher. It would do this by experience-rating each participant, that is, determining an individual's expected healthcare costs under the basic MSS policy. The experience rating would be done on an annual basis. Hence, if a participant's health deteriorated over the course of the year, thereby raising her future expected healthcare costs, she'd receive a larger voucher for the following year. And vice versa. Each and every factor relevant to a participant's expected healthcare costs would be used in determining each participant's voucher, including the participant's preexisting conditions, region (since healthcare costs differ regionally), age, sex, current medication regime, latest medical tests, current diagnoses, past medical history, and family medical history.

The MSS plan is highly progressive. The poor, who are more prone to illness than the rich, would on average receive higher vouchers than the rich. And because we'd be eliminating the deductibility of health insurance premium payments, the tax breaks going disproportionately to the rich in the form of non-taxed health insurance premium payments would vanish.

All medical information (for example, test results, diagnoses, and medical histories) would be transmitted electronically to the government for purposes of its experience rating. The confidentiality of these medical records would be strictly maintained. The insurer one picked would, of course, learn the size of one's voucher. In this way, the insurer would be able to infer the client's true expected healthcare costs. Hence, the insurer would, in effect, receive the information that would not be available in a standard insurance setting. The insurer would be required to keep this information confidential.

Can we trust the government to keep these records safe? Absolutely. The government has been keeping medical records in the strictest confidence since 1967 for tens of millions of Medicaid and Medicare participants. Medicare, for example, knows the hospital diagnosis-related groups against which it has been paying claims for each of its participants. It also knows a host of other information about individuals, such as which doctors they see on an outpatient basis for what conditions. It certainly isn't reporting any of this information to the local newspaper.

The key thing from a cost perspective is that the government can establish the values of the vouchers each year such that its total expenditure on vouchers per MSS beneficiary grows only as fast as per capita national income. This would slice tens of trillions of dollars off our $70 trillion fiscal gap.

Yes, Medicare participants would no longer be able to look forward to growth in real medical benefits that far outstrips the growth in the nation's per capita income, but those benefit hikes are no longer affordable. Today's elderly, like everyone else, will, however, be able to look forward to benefits rising at the same rate as per capita income, which is significant in its own right. Furthermore, today's elderly will be able to sleep at night knowing they are no longer participating in a healthcare system that is facing financial ruin.

All insurers, HMOs, and health plans that wished to enroll MSS participants would be required to cover the government-determined set of basic benefits, including prescription drug coverage and nursing home care. But the insurers would be free to provide rebates to participants in exchange for including copayments and deductibles in their policies that would limit their use of the healthcare system. The insurers could also provide monetary rewards for healthy behavior, such as losing weight, smoking less or not at all, and going to the gym regularly. Such arrangements would be subject to government approval.

In determining on an annual basis the set of medical goods and services that the basic policy would have to cover, the government would clearly be rationing healthcare or, at least, the healthcare that it is willing to pay for. But insurers would be free to offer supplemental or major medical policies that cover medical goods and services that are not covered under the basic policy, such as a private hospital room.

Such supplemental policies raise their own adverse selection concerns. For example, suppose your health is such that you have a high chance of being hospitalized in the next year. Also suppose you want to purchase a supplemental insurance policy that covers you for the cost of a private hospital room, should you in fact need to be hospitalized. If you are free to buy this policy from any insurer, your own primary insurer, which has inside information about you, may explicitly or subtly encourage you to purchase the supplemental policy from a different insurer. To avoid this problem, the MSS would require that any supplemental policy be purchased from only the primary insurer.

Restraining Healthcare Costs

At the margin, insurers and HMOs, not Uncle Sam and Aunt Sally, would be on the hook to pay for MSS participants' healthcare. Hence, they'd have a strong profit motive to find ways to tailor their insurance policies and contracts with hospitals and healthcare professionals to limit costs.

Although policies would differ from insurer to insurer, the government would develop and require a single electronic system of insurance record keeping and reporting. This, by itself, could squeeze out huge amounts of wasted administrative costs from our healthcare system. Another important reform is placing reasonable limits on malpractice liability, which will limit defensive medicine and represent another major cost saver.

MSS versus Universal Healthcare Vouchers

The MSS proposal is essentially identical to the universal health-care vouchers (UHV) plan, but there are three differences worth mentioning. First, MSS avoids adverse selection by experience-rating each individual separately and compensating each individual in terms of the size of his or her voucher for preexisting medical conditions. Hence, insurers and HMOs will no longer have an incentive to cherry-pick participants; that is, their sickest participants will present as fine a profit opportunity as their healthiest.[4] In contrast, UHV appears to do its experience rating at the level of the insurer or HMO. This would, I believe, be much less accurate because it wouldn't make use of all available participant-specific data. Therefore, it may still leave insurers and HMOs with strong incentives to find subtle and not-so-subtle ways to avoid insuring the sickest members of society. But there is nothing in the UHV proposal to limit the government in the information it uses to experience-rate the insurer or HMO. The UHV plan could simply entail the government's experience-rating the insurer or HMO by experience-rating each of its customers or participants on an individual-specific basis.

Second, UHV calls for a value-added tax (an indirect way to tax consumption) to finance the costs of its vouchers. I don't believe major additional revenues would be needed for MSS. But careful study would be required to determine whether this is the case. Were additional revenues needed, I too would favor using a consumption tax, but I'd advocate a progressive federal retail sales tax. Indeed, I propose replacing our entire federal tax system with a federal retail sales tax that includes a monthly rebate.[5] The third difference, and this one is major, is that UHV would leave Medicare in place for all existing Medicare participants. This option is simply unaffordable. Medicare on its own is fully capable of sinking our fiscal ship, and its spending must be brought under control. Furthermore, there is no reason to treat the elderly any different from the rest of the population in terms of the quality of their healthcare.

Paying for the Medical Security System

Government—federal, state, and local—is currently responsible for 60 percent of total national health expenditures.[6] This 60 percent figure includes not only direct expenditures on Medicare, Medicaid, workers' compensation, the Department of Veterans Affairs, public hospitals, and government public health activities. It also includes what now amounts to over $200 billion in so-called tax expenditures.[7] In this context, tax expenditures reference the loss of federal income and payroll tax revenue and state and local income tax revenue due to the exemption of employer-paid health insurance premiums as well as a range of tax breaks provided for employee-paid health insurance premiums.

Over time the government's share of total U.S. healthcare spending will rise significantly for four reasons. The first involves the recently enacted Medicare Part D prescription drug benefit. Expenditures on Part D net of participant and state premium payments are slated to grow rapidly over time owing to projected increases in enrollment and increases in the costs of prescription medications.[8]

The second reason is demographic. Recall that compared with health expenditure in general, government healthcare spending is concentrated on the elderly. Eighty-four percent of Medicare participants are aged, with the remainder being disabled workers, most of whom are also older workers. As for Medicaid, although three-quarters of its enrollees are children and their parents, 70 percent of Medicaid spending is on elderly and disabled participants, most of whom are at least middle-aged. Consequently, as the nation ages, Medicare and Medicaid spending will rise as a share of national health expenditures.

A third factor is the likely further decline in employer-provided health insurance coverage. Employers are slowly, but it appears surely, getting out of the health insurance business, which is one of the main reasons that the ranks of the uninsured swelled by over 7 million between 2000 and 2007.[9] As the number of the uninsured continues to expand, more and more of the responsibility of covering their healthcare costs will fall on Medicaid as well as the largesse of public hospitals and clinics. Recall that in recent years most of Medicaid expenditure growth has been driven by increases in enrollment. Between 2000 and 2003, for example, the number of families enrolled in Medicaid grew by 19.5 percent.[10]

A fourth factor is the ongoing rise in income inequality. Between 1980 and 2000, the share of pretax income received by the 1 percent of Americans with the highest pretax incomes rose from 8 percent to 14 percent.[11] Since higher-income Americans are in higher tax brackets and have relatively more expensive health insurance policies, increases in income inequality mean increases in the size of overall federal and state health-related tax expenditures—the income and payroll tax breaks associated with employer-paid and, to a lesser extent, employee-paid health insurance premiums.

What do these four factors imply for the likely rise in the government share of overall health expenditures? My reading of projections of the Centers for Medicare and Medicaid Services (CMS);[12] my consultation with economist John Shields, who has done a careful recent study of healthcare tax expenditures; and my consideration of trends in health insurance coverage and employer-provided health insurance suggest that the government share of total U.S. health expenditures will rise from its current roughly 60 percent value to 70 percent within a decade. This means that in the short term, government healthcare spending would need to rise by only 43 percent (30 percent divided by 70 percent) were the government to pay for all current U.S. healthcare expenditures. But this overstates the requisite short-term rise in government spending under the MSS plan for two reasons. First, only about 90 percent of national healthcare expenditures represent expenditures that would need to be covered by the MSS plan. For example, the MSS plan would not cover routine dental care, plastic surgery, or nonprescription medications. Nor would it need to cover private healthcare investment, such as the purchase of new MRIs or the construction of new hospitals.

Second, there is surely another 10 percent of costs that can be wrung out of the system by having a uniform method of administering and insuring for healthcare. Indeed, of every dollar now spent on U.S. healthcare, some 20 to 30 percent appears to be spent on bureaucracy and administration.[13] The typical U.S. hospital spends a quarter of its budget on billing and administration, which has, as far as one can tell, no curative powers.

Once one adjusts for the healthcare spending that would not need to be covered by MSS and accounts for administrative saving, it appears that what our government (broadly defined) will likely spend on healthcare in the short term would cover almost 90 percent of what the MSS would cost.

Galvanizing Political Support

Fourteen years have passed since our nation last seriously debated healthcare reform. But the issue is once again front and center. The reason is clear. Our healthcare system is making everyone sick—sick with fear. Forty-seven million uninsured Americans are living every day with overwhelming anxiety that they'll get sick and have to hand over their life's savings to pay their medical bills. Millions of insured workers live with the gnawing fear that they could be next—next to lose their insurance coverage because the company either cancels the policy or simply lets them go. And millions of elderly go to bed at night worrying whether Medicare is running short of money, whether they'll be able to afford Medicare's soaring premiums, whether their doctors will drop them because of Medicare's low reimbursement rates, and, heaven forbid, whether they will end up like so many others: living in a nursing home, flat broke, and at the mercy of Medicaid.

This system stinks. There's no other way to put it. And suddenly, everybody seems to realize it.

To me the parameters for change are clear. We need a single, efficient, transparent system that includes everyone, that treats everyone fairly, that covers all the basics, including prescription drugs, home healthcare, and nursing home care, and that costs no more than the economy can afford.

Is this vision utopian? Can we get everyone to support a single system? Will the elderly give up Medicare? Will the employed give up their employer's plans? I believe the answer is yes, for a simple reason. The current system is generating so much anxiety that everyone—young and old, rich and poor—has more to gain than to lose from switching to the MSS.

This point came home to me in spades when I attended a recent conference of AGE—Americans for Generational Equity. The keynote speaker was former Supreme Court Justice Sandra Day O'Connor, who spoke with great passion and at length about her own family's healthcare problems. I did not take notes and was listening more to the anguish in her voice than to the details of her son's loss of health insurance. But the gist of what I heard was that the justice's son had lost excellent coverage from previous employment and was now uninsured and unable to get coverage for his family because of a preexisting health condition of one of his children—the justice's grandchild.

"Why can't a country as rich and talented and resourceful as ours provide basic health insurance to everyone?" This was the justice's closing question. The fact that she was asking it, not just for others, but also for herself, and for her son, and for her grandchild was to me quite astonishing. My Lord, I thought, no one is immune from our nation's healthcare problems. They are literally affecting everyone, and the system has to change.

Of course, I may be politically naive. Certainly, one anonymous reviewer of this book's proposal thought so. He wrote

The specific plan is technically feasible, but in my view is extremely politically naive, as the voucher-centeredness will offend the Democrats and the centralization of power and information will offend the Republicans. Like so many academic musings, it is written as if one could plausibly write off the current US health care system which disposes of as much money as the combined GNPs of France and Spain and the myriad interests that this money represents without paying any attention to the starting point, which is the system we have . . .

Fortunately, the other reviewers were much more favorable; otherwise, you'd not be reading this book. But this passage is worth consideration, starting with "voucher-centeredness will offend the Democrats." Frankly, I'm not sure why giving everyone a voucher, with the size of the voucher being larger the higher your expected healthcare costs, would offend anyone, let alone Democrats. Perhaps the concern here is with the word "voucher." Many democrats take great issue with school vouchers, so the word "voucher" seems to be highly charged. My other candidates for this instrument were "coupon," "certificate," "grant," "health stamps," and "health check." In the end, I thought it best to use "voucher" because I knew that whatever I called it, others would call it "voucher" and then experience whatever visceral reaction that word engenders.

If you, my reader, don't like that word, please try my alternatives. But also please look through the language to the substance of what is being proposed. After all, food stamps could well be called food vouchers, and doing so would make no difference to this system of nutritional support of the poor. Likewise Medicare benefits could be called health vouchers, perhaps with the government mailing the voucher to the patient who then forwards it to the provider. Even Social Security benefits could be relabeled old age vouchers with absolutely no alteration in the system's functioning or mission.

The problem is too serious to be hobbled by word choice. Substance we can and must debate. But semantics must simply get out of the way.

The second critique of the review is that "the centralization of power and information will offend the Republicans." This, too, I find hard to follow. Republicans have supported Medicare and Medicaid for decades even though these programs centralize information about and centralize power over what is approaching one-third of the population. Republicans also support the IRS, which centralizes information and power over virtually the entire adult population.

At least one Republican, Justice O'Connor, wasn't taken aback by the MSS proposal to have a single government healthcare information system whose main purpose is to protect those with bad information—preexisting conditions—from being penalized in purchasing a health plan in the marketplace. I was, you see, the second speaker after Justice O'Connor at the conference and had the opportunity to present the MSS plan to her and the other attendees and then briefly discuss the plan with her during the break. No one recorded our conversation, but the justice was very encouraging and seemed not the least bit concerned about the government's knowing for the entire population what it already knows for one-third of the population.

The third concern of the reviewer is that "[the MSS]) . . . write(s) off the current US health care system. . . ." Not so. The MSS maintains and strengthens our system of private medicine as well as private health plans, whether they be called private health insurance policies, private health plans, or private HMOs. Yes, the MSS plan writes off tax breaks for the purchase of private health insurance. But it doesn't write off private insurance. Instead, it provides everyone with vouchers to buy private insurance (i.e., a health plan issued by a private insurer) and makes sure that no one's prior health conditions will be used against them when it comes to interacting in this private market. And yes, the MSS plan writes off Medicare and Medicaid, but it doesn't write off their goals. Instead, it applies their objectives to the entire population while meeting these objectives in a much more efficient and straightforward manner.

In sum, I don't believe I'm naive. Rather I believe the time is ripe for a broad healthcare compact. But achieving this compact will require every American to think outside the current healthcare box and examine the substance of what is being proposed and ignore its nomenclature.

Thanks to decades of fiscal profligacy and the impending retirement of the baby boom generation, the United States is essentially bankrupt and requires critical and immediate fiscal surgery. The single greatest threat to our nation's finances is the government's runaway spending on Medicare and Medicaid. The decades-long explosion in Medicare and Medicaid expenditures reflects real benefit levels that have been rising at a much faster clip than real income per capita, the expansion of the programs to cover ever more medical goods and services, and major growth in enrollments.

The financial markets have yet to see the fire at the end of this tunnel, but it's there and burning ever brighter. Unless we immediately and radically change direction, it will be too late. Seventy-seven million baby boomers will retire and become accustomed to receiving ever higher benefits, notwithstanding the economic toll this will place on the economy and on their children. Unfortunately, neither Republican nor Democratic politicians are offering medicine strong enough to cure this patient. Indeed, many of their proposals will make the overall cost problem much worse.

The MSS proposal I offer here is simple, straightforward, and foolproof. Whatever the government decides it can afford to spend on the public's health, it simply hands out in the form of universal health insurance vouchers. MSS entails a single payer, but it's not a single payer for healthcare; it's a single payer for health insurance. The U.S. healthcare industry will remain competitive, innovative, strong, and private.

The MSS is not a form of socialized medicine. It is first and foremost a plan for universal health insurance. Because everyone will be insured, there will also be universal healthcare. But make no mistake, our nation already has universal healthcare, and our government already pays for the vast majority of it explicitly or implicitly through tax breaks and other means.

In this concise book I have tried to help the reader see the forest for the trees, specifically to show that our country's current version of universal healthcare is a haphazard, inefficient, and incredibly costly means of meeting our paternalistic imperatives. It's time to make a major fix—retire Medicare and Medicaid, and put in place one system that works for everyone and will help secure our nation's fiscal, economic, and medical futures.

Glossary

Adverse selection   using private information in choosing insurers or insurees.

Asymmetry of information   differences in information among market participants concerning the product being purchased.

Diagnosis-related group   the classification of medical care recipients by the nature of their ailments.

Experience rating   determining the expected costs of insuring an individual or group.

Fee for service   the payment by the government of fees charged for medical services provided to Medicare and Medicaid participants.

Fiscal gap   the value today (the present value) of all future projected government expenditures less all future projected government receipts.

Gross domestic product (GDP)   the value of a nation's production of final goods and services in a given year.

Health savings account   a savings account whose contributions are tax deductible and whose outlays must be used for healthcare.

Hillary Care   a proposal for universal healthcare developed during the Clinton administration by Hillary Rodham Clinton.

Hyperinflation   an extremely high and often rising rate of inflation.

Inferior good   a good or service that garners a smaller share of households' budgets as their incomes rise.

Inflation   a general rise in prices over a fixed period of time.

Lemons market   an insurance market in which only those at most risk are covered because of adverse selection.

Medicaid   the U.S. government's program of medical assistance to the poor, including paying for the nursing home costs of the poor elderly.

Medical Security System (MSS)   the universal health insurance voucher system proposed in this book.

Medicare   the U.S. government's program of medical assistance to the elderly.

MSS   See Medical Security System.

National income   the sum of all the labor and asset income earned worldwide by a country's population before any taxes are paid or government transfer payments are received.

Per capita gross domestic product   a country's national gross domestic product divided by its population size.

Per capita income   a country's national income divided by its population size.

Present value   the value today of money either received or paid in the future.

Progressivity   a fiscal system that (1) increases the ratio of tax payments to income and (2) reduces the ratio of transfer payments to income as income rises.

Prospective payment system   classifying each patient as falling into a diagnosis-related group (DRG) and giving the hospital a fixed amount of money for that DRG.

SCHIP   See State Child Health Insurance Program.

State Child Health Insurance Program (SCHIP)   a federal program enacted in 1997 to provide more health insurance coverage to children.

Superior good   a good or service that garners a larger share of households' budgets as their incomes rise.

Notes

Chapter 1

1. Medicare provides healthcare to the elderly, and Medicaid provides healthcare to the poor, including the nursing home care of poor elderly. In the case of the elderly, Medicaid's major expenditure is nursing home care. The Medicaid expenditures included in the definition of MSS are those spent on the elderly, which constitute 70 percent of the total. MMS benefits are measured gross of Medicare premiums.

2. Per capita income is measured as national income divided by the size of the population.

3. These and related calculations are the author's and are based on Congressional Budget Office reports of historic and projected expenditures and on U.S. Census past and projected demographic data.

4. See Christian Hagist and Laurence J. Kotlikoff, "Who's Going Broke? Comparing Healthcare Costs in Ten OECD Countries" (National Bureau of Economic Research working paper 11833, December 2005). Benefit level refers to average benefit paid per person in a given age group. Increasing Medicare or Medicaid coverage among people of a given age as well as raising the benefits paid to those already covered jointly explain the increases over time in benefit levels.

5. Part of the benefit increase referenced here reflects increases in Medicare and Medicare coverage rates.

6. See Office of the President, *Economic Report of the President* (Washington, D.C.: U.S. Government Printing Office, 2006), table B49, p. 340.

7. See ibid., table B47, p. 338.

8. Paul Fronstin, testimony before the U.S. House, Committee on Ways and Means, Subcommittee on Health, *Hearing on Health Insurance Coverage and Uninsured Americans*, April 4, 2001, available at http://www.ebri.org/pdf/publications/testimony/T126.pdf.

9. Paul Krugman, "A Healthy New Year," *New York Times*, January 1, 2007, p. 23.

10. Bob Herbert, "Your Master Card or Your Life," *New York Times*, January 22, 2007, p. 23.

11. See the official Web site of the Massachusetts Office of Consumer Affairs and Business Regulation, http:/www.mass.gov/?pageID=ocatopic&L=3&L0=Home&L1=Consumer&L2=Insurance&sid=Eoca.

12. Henry J. Kaiser Foundation, "Survey of Employer Health Benefits 2006" (Menlo Park, Calif.: Henry J. Kaiser Foundation, 2006), available at http://www.kff.org/insurance/7527/upload/7561.pdf.

13. John Sheils and Randall Haught, "The Cost of Tax-Exempt Benefits in 2004," *Health Affairs*, February 25, 2004, pp. 106-112, available at http://content.healthaffairs.org/cgi/reprint/hlthaff.w4.106v1.pdf.

14. Ford Motor Co. Web site, "Health Care Costs Affect Our Competitiveness, http://www.ford.com/en/company/about/sustainability/report/finCosts.htm.

15. General Motors Web site, News & Issues, "GM and UAW Reach Tentative Agreement on Healthcare," http://www.gm.com/company/gmability/workplace/100_news/120_news/uaw_101705.html.

16. Lisa Clemans-Cope, Bowen Gareett, and Catherine Hoffman, "Changes in Employees' Health Insurance Coverage, 2000–2005, Kaiser Commission on Medicaid and the Uninsured, October 2006, http://www .kff.org/uninsured/upload/7570.pdf.

17. Robert Wood Johnson Foundation, "Report Shows Decline in Employees Accepting Health Insurance, Rising Premiums Across the Nation, May 4, 2006, Washington, D.C., http://www.rwjf.org/newsroom/news releasesdetail.jsp?id=10408.

18. Present value is the value now (in the present) of money received or paid in the future. If the interest rate is 10 percent, the present value of $110 paid or received a year from now is $100 since one can invest $100 now and have $110 in a year.

19. During 2002 Gokhale was working at the Treasury while on leave from the Federal Reserve Bank of Cleveland. Their most recent fiscal gap study is Jagadeesh Gokhale and Kent Smetters, "Measuring Social Security's Financial Problems" (National Bureau of Economic Research working paper 11060, January 2005).

20. Ron Suskind, *The Price of Loyalty: George W. Bush, the White House, and the Education of Paul O'Neill* (New York: Simon & Schuster, 2004).

21. Jagadeesh Gokhale and Kent Smetters, *Fiscal and Generational Imbalances: New Budget Measures for New Budget Priorities* (Washington, D.C.: American Enterprise Institute, 2003).

22. Together with Scott Burns, I proposed the MSS plan in our recent book, *The Coming Generational Storm* (Cambridge, Mass.: MIT Press, 2004). As we indicated in the book, the essence of the plan was originally conceived by economists Peter Ferrara at the Institute for Policy Innovation and John Goodman, president of the National Center for Policy Analysis. Oncologist Ezekiel Emanuel and economist Victor R. Fuchs proposed essentially the same reform in "Solved!" *Washington Monthly*, June 2005. See http://www.washingtonmonthly.com/features/2005/0506.emanuel

.html. Niall Ferguson and I also advanced the plan in "Benefits without Bankruptcy: The New Deal," *New Republic*, August 15, 2005, pp. 18–21.

Chapter 2

1. These tables and this chapter draw heavily on Christian Hagist and Laurence J. Kotlikoff, "Who's Going Broke? Comparing Healthcare Costs in Ten OECD Countries" (National Bureau of Economic Research working paper 11833, December 2005).

2. Naoki Ikegami and John Creighton Campbell, "Japan's Health Care System: Containing Costs and Attempting Reform," *Health Affairs* 23, no. 3 (2004): 26–36.

3. Gene Sperling is the "economist" primarily responsible for this censuring of OMB's generational accounting analysis, which I helped coauthor. Sperling now claims to be seriously concerned about the nation's long-term fiscal problems; see his "The Buck Stops Where?" *Blueprint*, September 25, 2002.

4. See Joseph P. Newhouse, "Medical Care Costs: How Much Welfare Loss?" *Journal of Economic Perspectives* 6, no. 3 (1992): 9–16; and Peter Zweifel, "Medical Innovation: A Challenge to Society and Insurance," *Geneva Papers on Risk and Insurance: Issues and Practice* 28, no. 2 (2002): 194–202.

5. As reported in Organization for Economic Coordination and Development, *Health Data 2004*, 3rd ed. (Paris: OECD, 2004).

6. See ibid.

7. For this point, see also Uwe E. Reinhardt, Peter S. Hussey, and Gerald F. Anderson, "Cross-National Comparisons Systems Using OECD Data," *Health Affairs* 21, no. 3 (2002): 169–181.

8. David Cutler and Mark McClellan, "Is Technological Change in Healthcare Worth It?" *Health Affairs* 20, no. 5 (2001): 11–29.

9. See Web site of Centers for Medicare and Medicaid Services, National Health Expenditures Data http://www.cms.hhs.gov/NationalHealth ExpendData/downloads/tables.pdf.

10. See table 3 in Kotlikoff and Hagist, "Who's Going Broke?"

11. For a discussion and an overview of several studies concerning income elasticities of healthcare expenditures, see Jennifer Roberts, "Sensitivity of Elasticity Estimates for OECD Healthcare Spending: Analysis of a Dynamic Heterogeneous Data Field," *Health Economics* 8, no. 5 (1999): 459–472.

12. For a family of four in 2006, the poverty line is $20,000 in annual income.

13. Jagadeesh Gokhale and Kent Smetters, *Fiscal and Generational Imbalances: New Budget Measures for New Budget Priorities* (Washington, D.C.: American Enterprise Institute, 2003).

14. For a good description of the German hyperinflation, see Adam Smith, *Paper Money* (New York: Summit Books, 1981).

15. See Web site of Government Accountability Office, selected presentations from the Comptroller General of the United States, David M. Walker, Saving Our Future Requires Tough Choices Today, Fiscal Wake-Up Tour at Denver City College, Denver, Colorado, November 28, 2006, GAO-07-269CG. See http://www.gao.gov/cghome.htm and testimony of Chairman Ben S. Bernanke, *Long-term fiscal challenges facing the United States,* before the Committee on the Budget, U.S. Senate, January 18, 2007, http://www .federalreserve.gov/boarddocs/testimony/2007/20070118/default.htm.

16. Author's calculations based on National Income and Product Account data.

Chapter 3

1. Kenneth E. Thorpe and David H. Howard, "The Rise in Spending Among Medicare Beneficiaries: The Role of Chronic Disease Prevalence

and Changes in Treatment Intensity," *Health Affairs* 25, no. 5 (2006): 378–388.

2. Medicare does, I presume, set some limits on extreme usage of the healthcare system. For example, it would certainly not pay for a colonoscopy every two weeks.

3. Jonathan Skinner and John E. Wennberg, "How Much Is Enough? Efficiency and Medicare Spending in the Last Six Months of Life," in David M. Cutler, ed., *The Changing Hospital Industry: Comparing Not-for-Profit and For-Profit Institutions* (Chicago: The University of Chicago Press, 2000), pp. 169–193.

4. See Centers for Medicare and Medicaid Web site, "Medicaid Managed Care Penetration: Rates and Expansion Enrollments by State," http://www.cms.hhs.gov/MedicaidDataSourcesGenInfo/

5. Programs oriented toward children, like SCHIP, indicate that there have been some important offsets to what has generally been an ongoing postwar policy of intergenerational expropriation of the young by the old.

Chapter 4

1. Steffie Woolhandler, Terry Campbell, and David U. Himmelstein, "Cost of Health Care Administration in the United States and Canada," *New England Journal of Medicine*, August 21, 2003, pp. 768–775.

2. Michael Tanner, "The 6.2 Percent Solution: A Plan for Reforming Social Security," Social Security Choice Paper, no. 32 (Washington, D.C.: Cato Institute, February 17, 2004).

3. See "Everybody In, Nobody Out," Web site posted at http://www.everybodyinnobodyout.org/DOCS/Polls.htm.

4. J. Buchanan, "The Samaritan's Dilemma," in E. Phelps (ed.), *Altruism, Morality, and Economic Theory* (New York: Russell Sage Foundation, 1975).

5. Paying other types of taxes can also be viewed as securing claims to future benefits because other taxes directly or indirectly finance these benefits; that is, a dollar's a dollar.

Chapter 5

1. Devon M. Herrick, "Update 2006: Why Are Health Costs Rising," Brief Analysis, no. 572 (Washington, D.C.: National Center for Policy Analysis, September 21, 2006), available at http://www.ncpa.org/pub/ba/ba572/.

2. Fraser, chapter 4, the St. Louis Federal Reserve Bank, http://fraser.stlouisfed.org/publications/ERP/issue/1600/download/6055/ERP1994_Chapter4.pdf.

3. Christopher Lee, "Massachusetts Begins Universal Healthcare," *Washington Post*, July 1, 2007.

4. The MSS proposal is included in *The Coming Generational Storm*, which I coauthored with Scott Burns (Cambridge, Mass.: MIT Press, 2004). I became aware of the Emanuel-Fuchs plan only recently in the course of doing research for this book. They appear to have developed their plan, which was first offered in an op-ed that appeared in the November–December 2003 issue of *Boston Review*, at roughly the same time I was working on the MSS proposal.

5. See, for example, Dunham, Morone, and White, "Restoring Medical Markets: Implications for the Poor," *Journal of Health Politics, Policy & Law*, 7:2 (Summer 1982).

6. Robert H. Frank, "A Health Care Plan So Simple, Even Stephen Colbert Couldn't Simplify," *New York Times*, February 15, 2007, http://www.rojo.com/story/QnlHllLVpXmOl_RYC_Single-Payer_Health_Care_and_Vouchers

7. The fact that both Goodman and Ferrara have strong libertarian leanings but nonetheless have spent considerable time considering how to

efficiently mandate universal healthcare is indicative that paternalism is alive and well among all segments of our society.

Chapter 6

1. George Will, "Bush's Bad News for the Right," *Boston Globe*, July 24, 2003, p. A11.

2. The Bush II administration, which has to approve these planned expansions of Medicaid's enrollment, appears disinclined to do so.

3. The public has, of course, taken some steps to improve its health, for example, reducing the prevalence of smoking.

4. The experience rating will need to be adjusted not just for differences across participants in expected healthcare costs, but also for differences in the distributions (riskiness) of those costs.

5. See Niall Ferguson and Laurence J. Kotlikoff, "Benefits Without Bankruptcy: The New New Deal," *New Republic*, August 18, 2005, pp. 18–21.

6. Asaf Bitton and James G, Kahn, "Government Share of Health Care Expenditures," *Journal of the American Medical Association*, June 26, 2007, p. 1165, available at http://jama.ama-assn.org/cgi/reprint/289/9/1165.pdf.

7. John Sheils and Randall Haught, "The Cost of Tax-Exempt Benefits in 2004," *Health Affairs*, February 25, 2004, pp. 106–112, available at http://content.healthaffairs.org/cgi/reprint/hlthaff.w4.106v1.pdf.

8. Over the next decade alone, the Congressional Budget Office forecasts that Medicare Part D net spending will rise from 0.3 to 0.8 percent of national income. http://www.cbo.gov/showdoc.cfm?index=6139&sequence=0.

9. Kaiser Commission on Medicaid Facts, "Medicaid and the Uninsured, Medicaid Enrollment and Spending Trends" June, 2005, available at

http://www.kff.org/medicaid/upload/Medicaid-Enrollment-and-Spend
ing-Trends-Fact-Sheet.pdf.

10. Ibid. My sense is that the Centers for Medicare and Medicaid Services
has not yet fully incorporated the imminent meltdown of employer-
provided health insurance in its Medicaid or Medicare spending projections.

11. Thomas Picketty and Emanuel Saez, "The Evolution of Top Incomes:
A Historical and International Perspective" (National Bureau of Economic Research working paper 11955, 2006).

12. See Centers for Medicare and Medicaid Web site, National Health
Expenditures   Projections,   2006–2016,   http://www.cms.hhs.gov/
NationalHealthExpendData/03_NationalHealthAccountsProjected
.asp#TopOfPage.

13. See Anna Bernasek, "Healthcare Problems? Check the American
Psyche," *New York Times*, December 31, 2006, available at http://www
.nytimes.com/2006/12/31/business/yourmoney/31view.html?page
wanted=2&ei=5088&en=3e09a7e6344af55a&ex=1325221200&partner
=rssnyt&emc=rss.

Index

The Medical Security System

1. Provides universal coverage.

2. Offers each American, annually, a health plan voucher.

3. Those with higher expected healthcare costs receive bigger vouchers.

4. Participants can change their health plans annually.

5. Government defines basic policy each year.

6. Basic policy covers drugs, home healthcare, and nursing home care.

7. Plans must cover basic policy.

8. Plans compete for participants.

9. Annual voucher budget is fixed as share of GDP.

10. Medicare, Medicaid, and employer-based health insurance tax breaks are eliminated.